WATERCOLOR DOGS

40 Beautiful Breeds

©2024. All rights reserved.

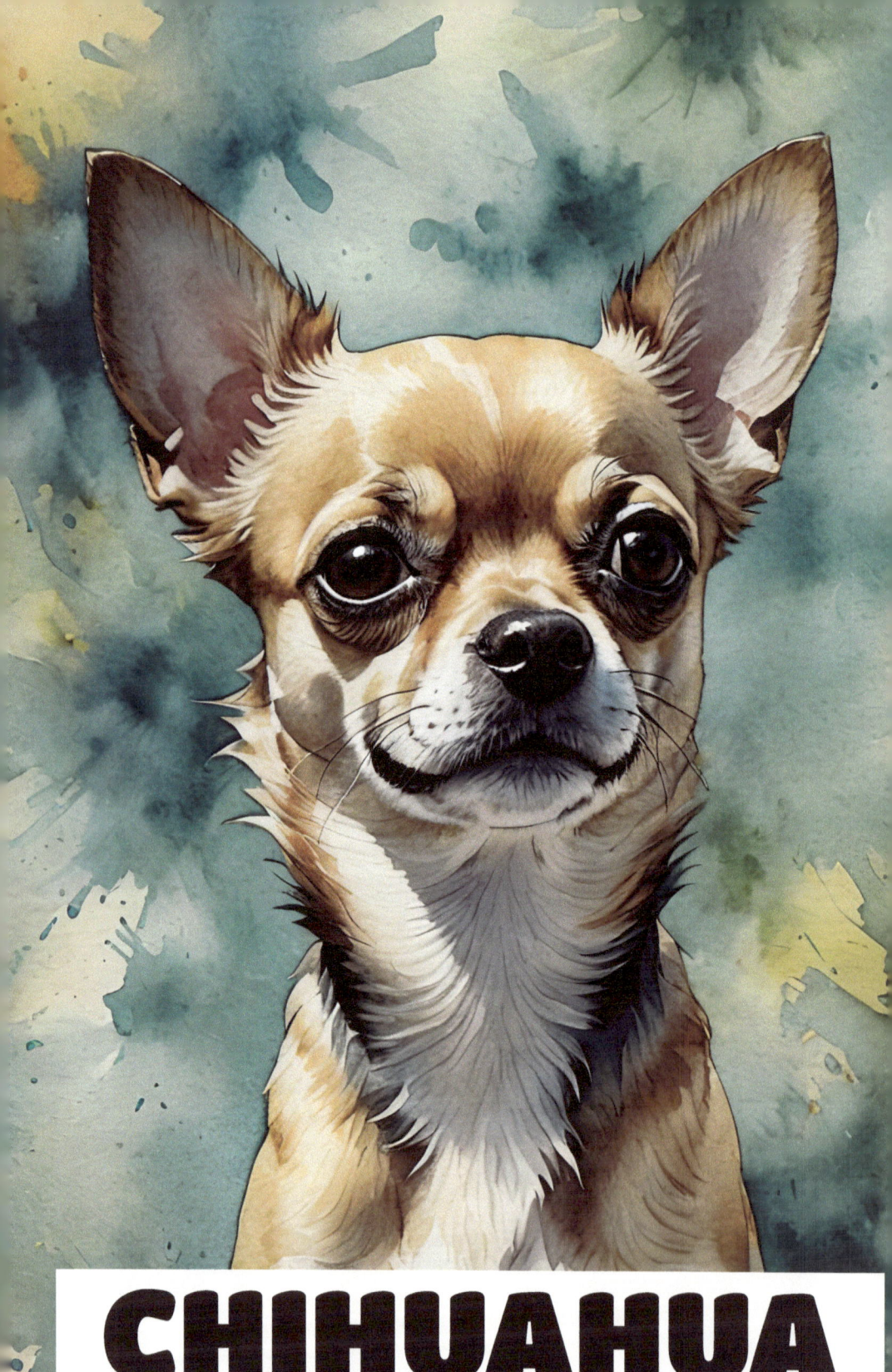

CHIHUAHUA

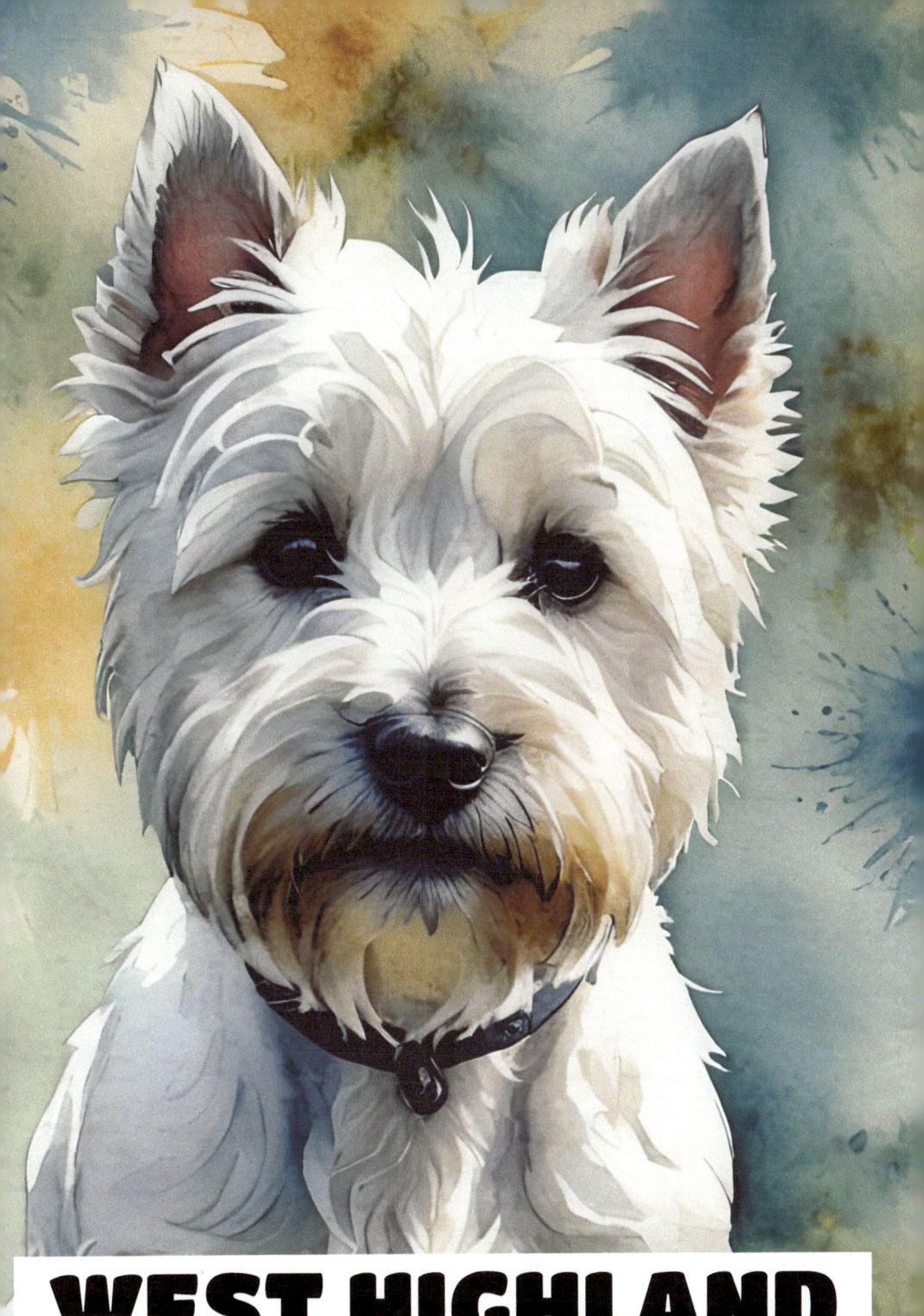

WEST HIGHLAND WHITE TERRIER

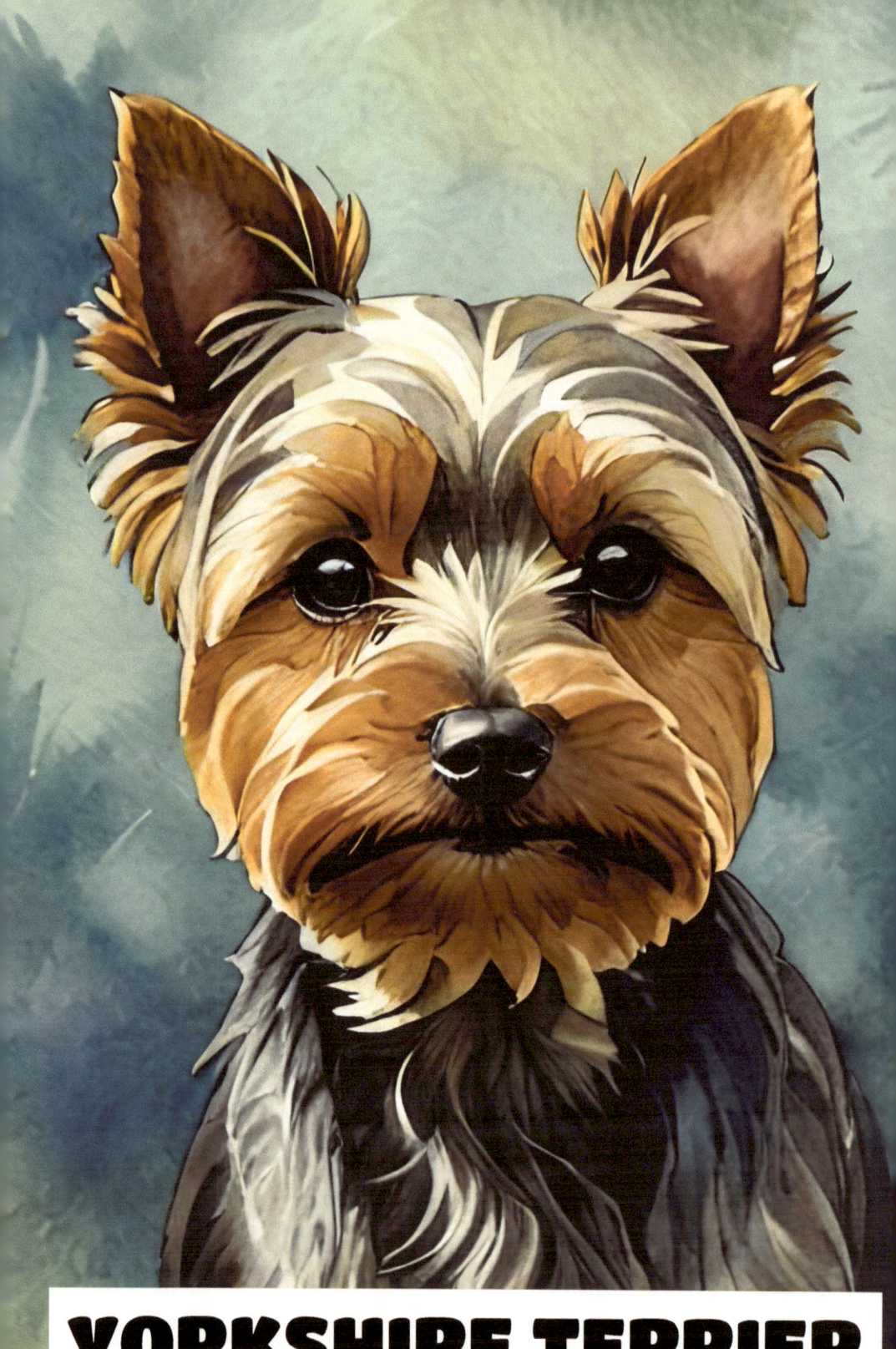

YORKSHIRE TERRIER

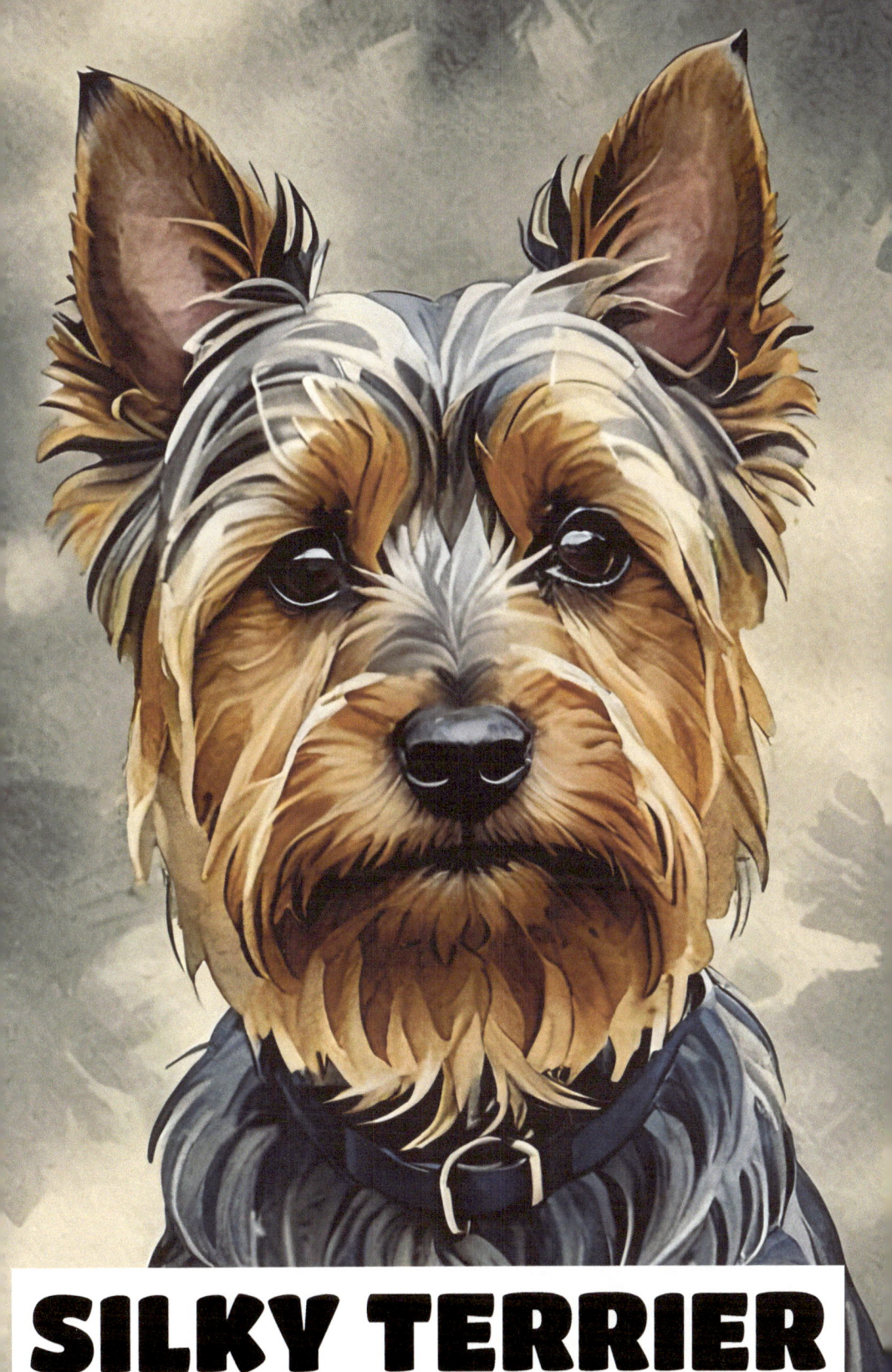

SILKY TERRIER

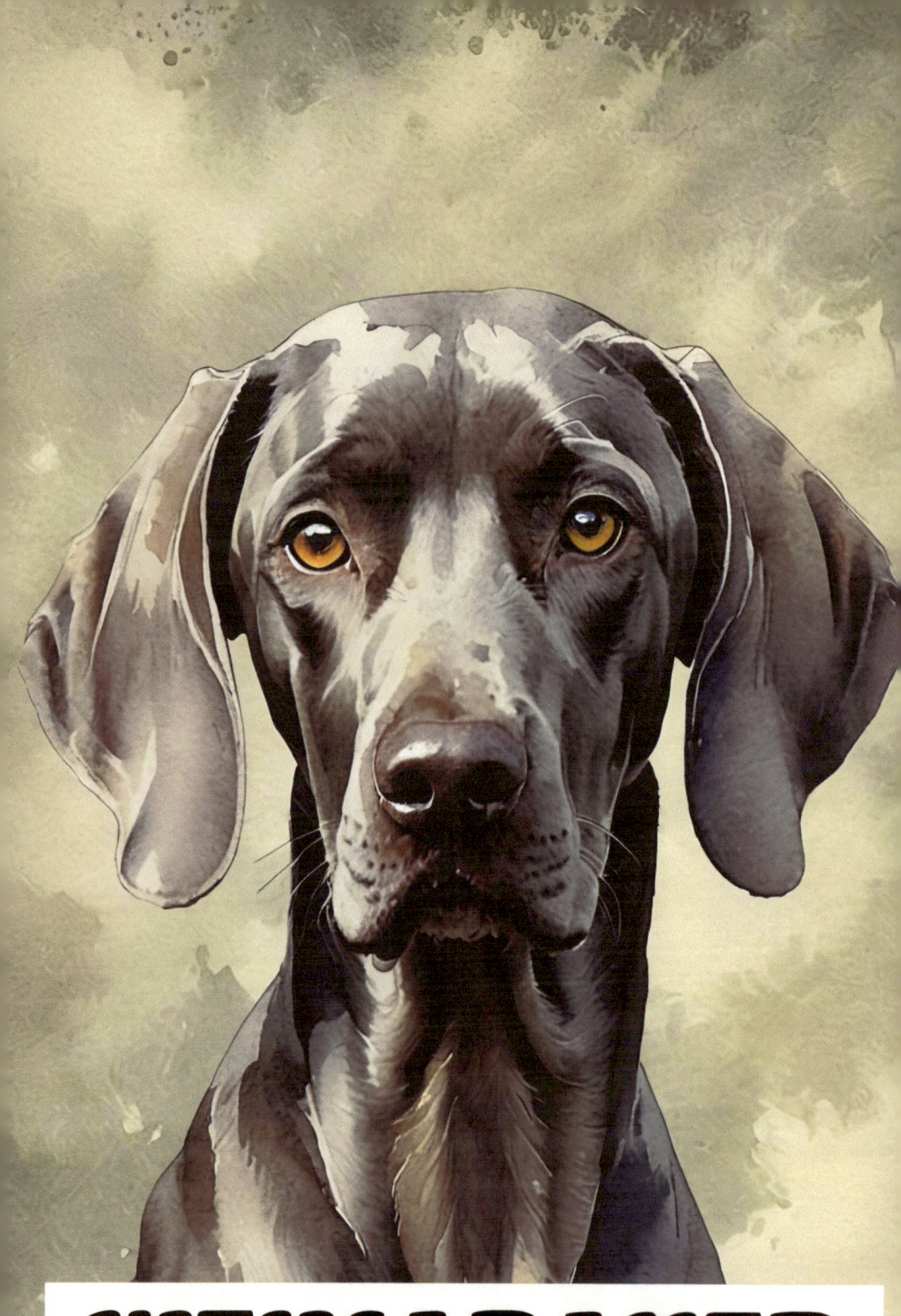

WEIMARANER

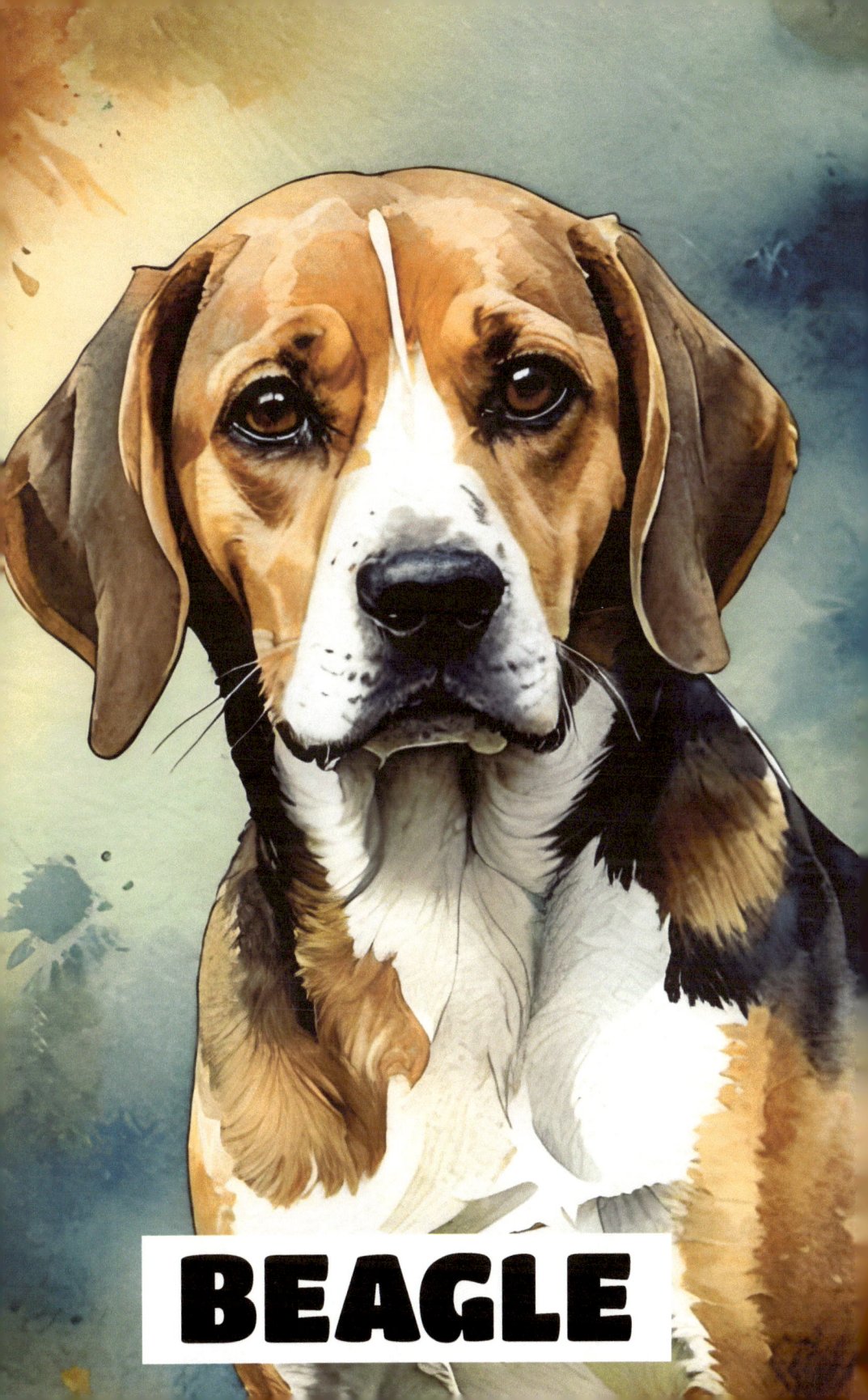

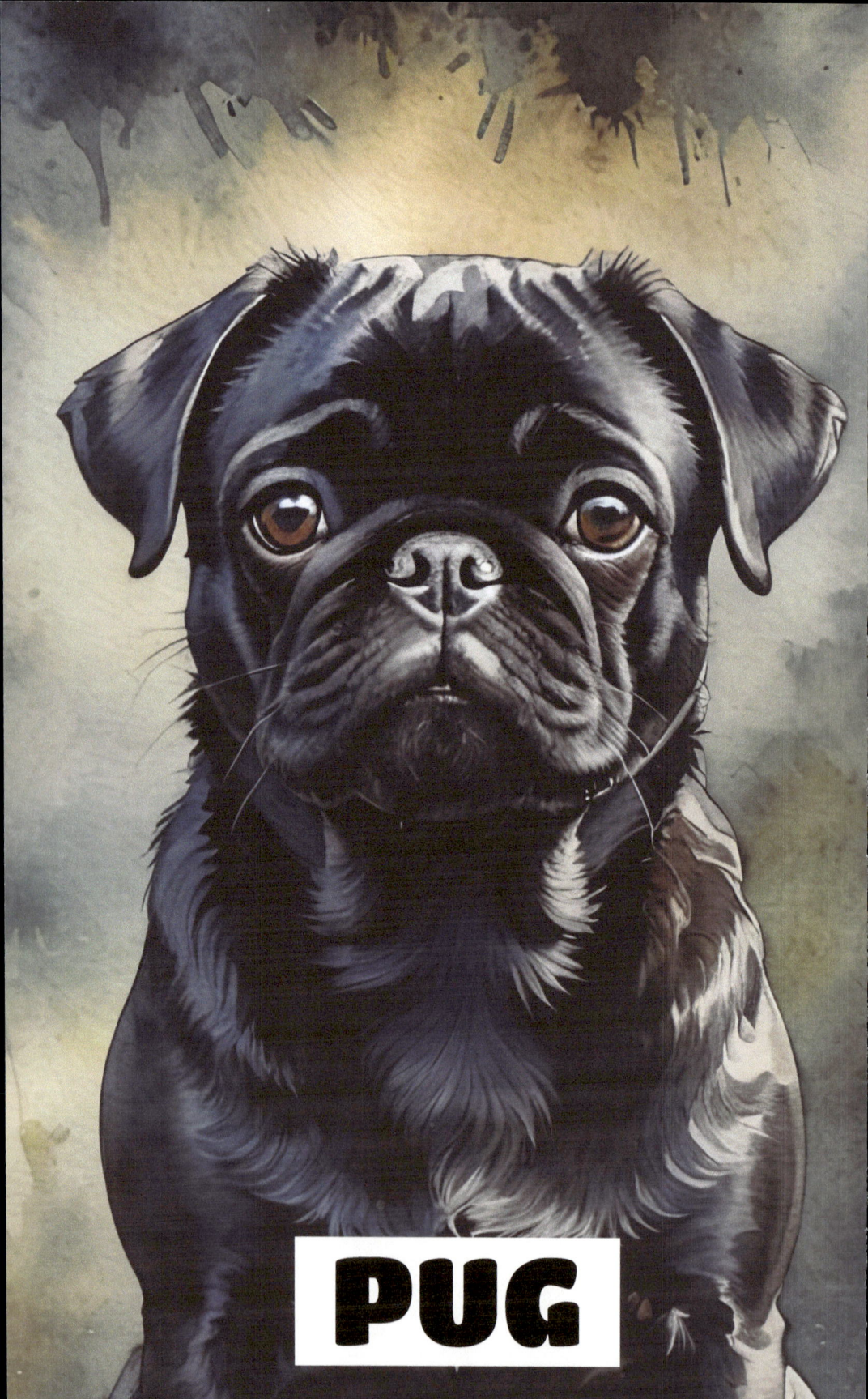

PUG

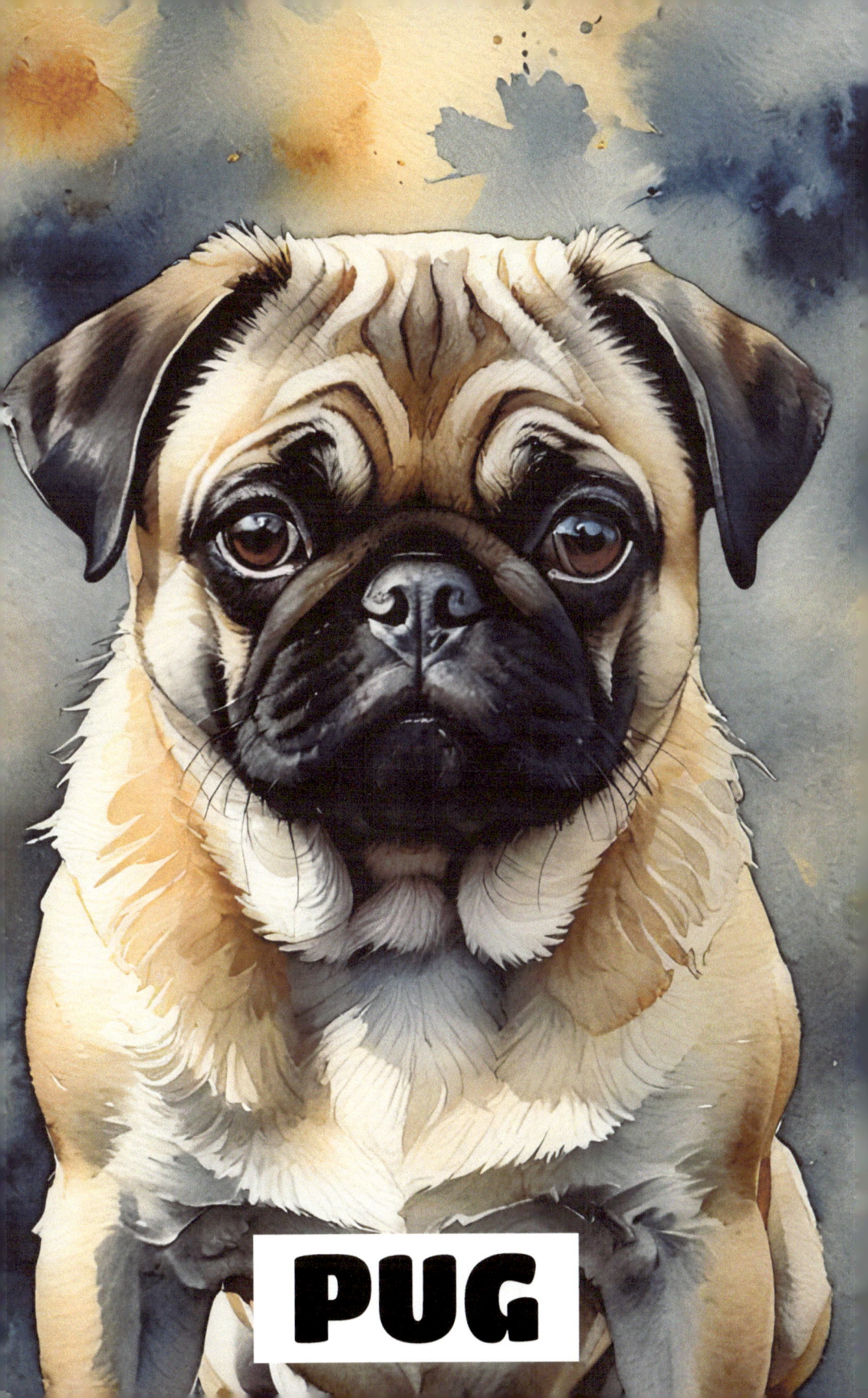

PUG

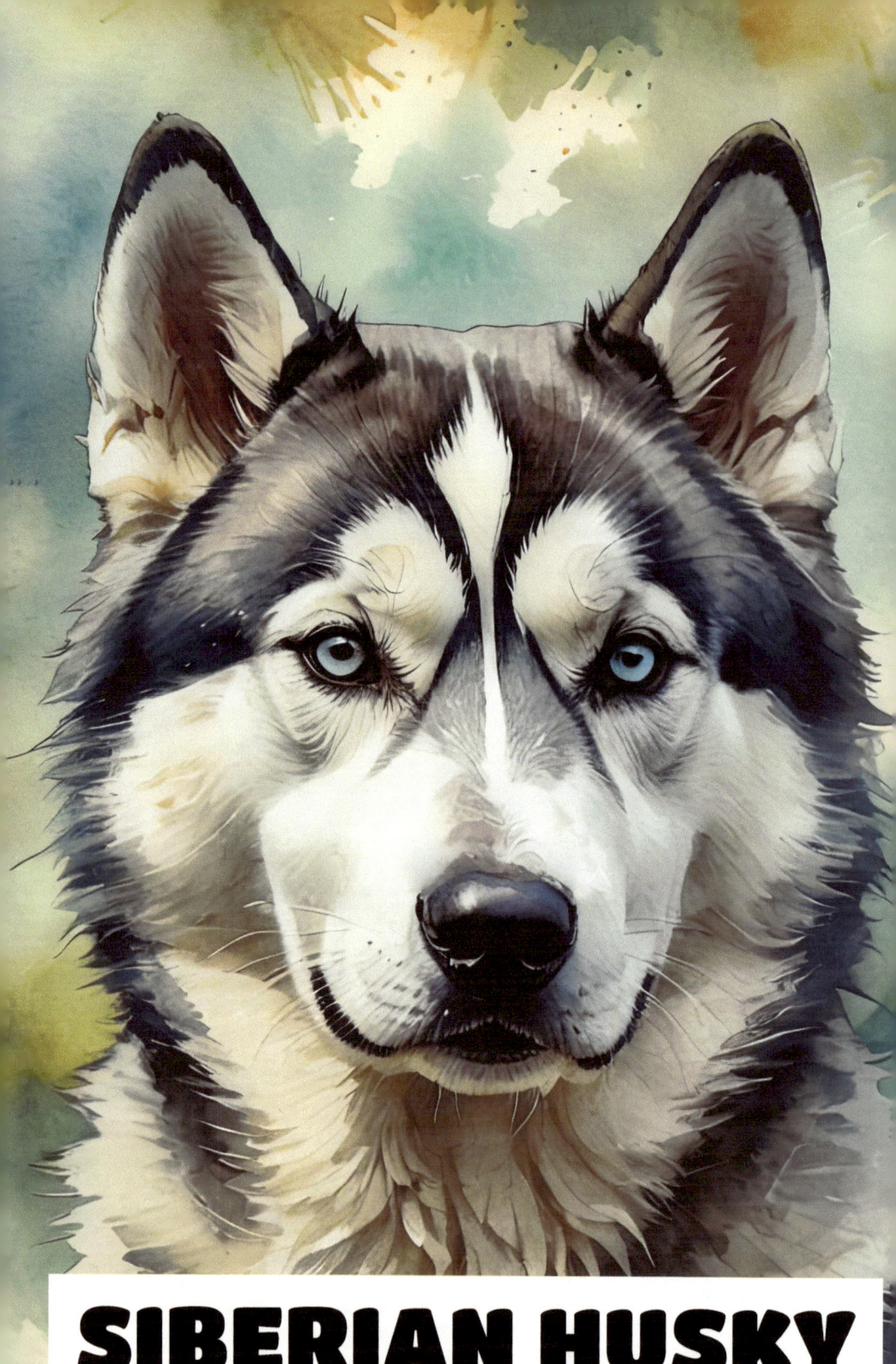

SIBERIAN HUSKY

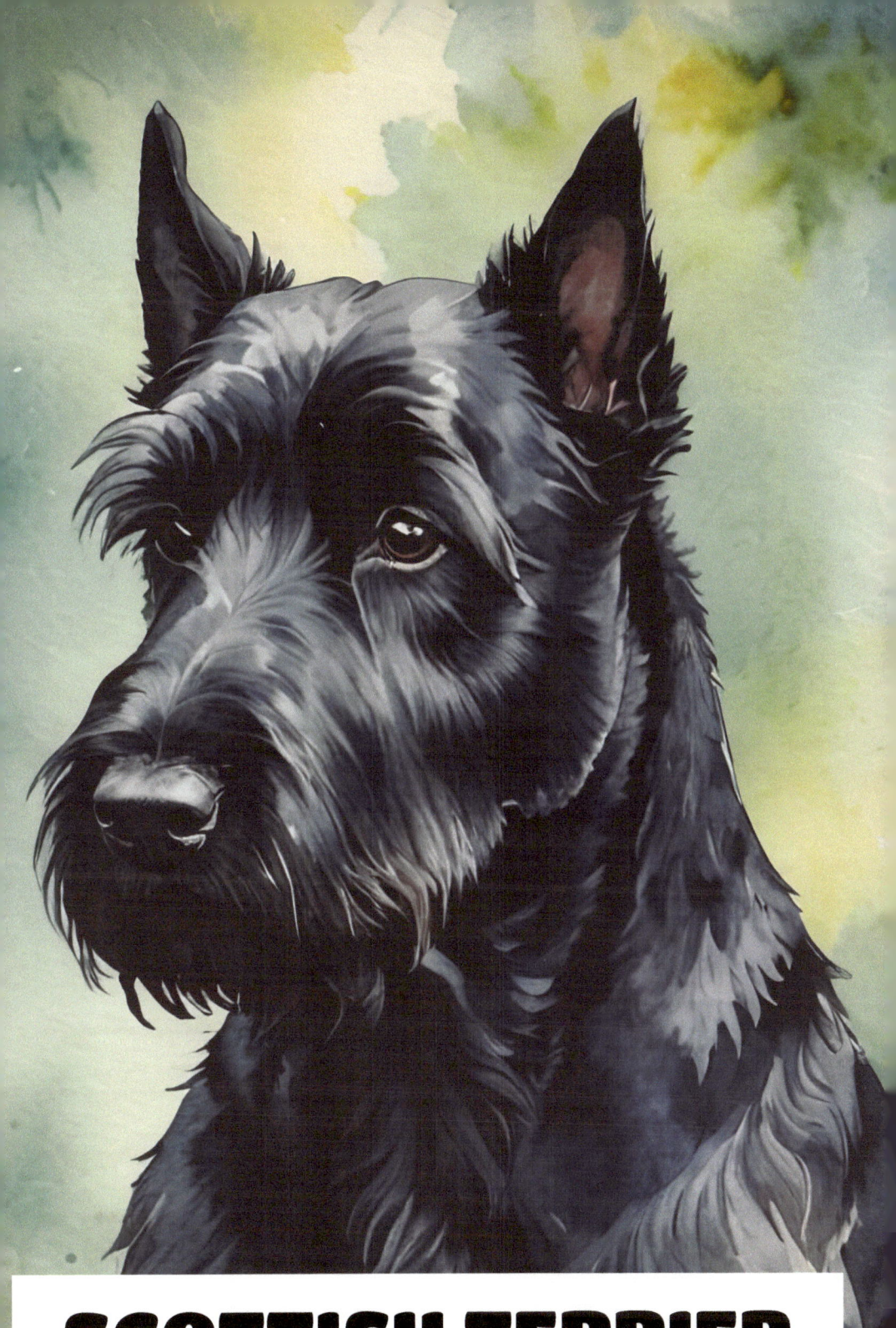

SCOTTISH TERRIER

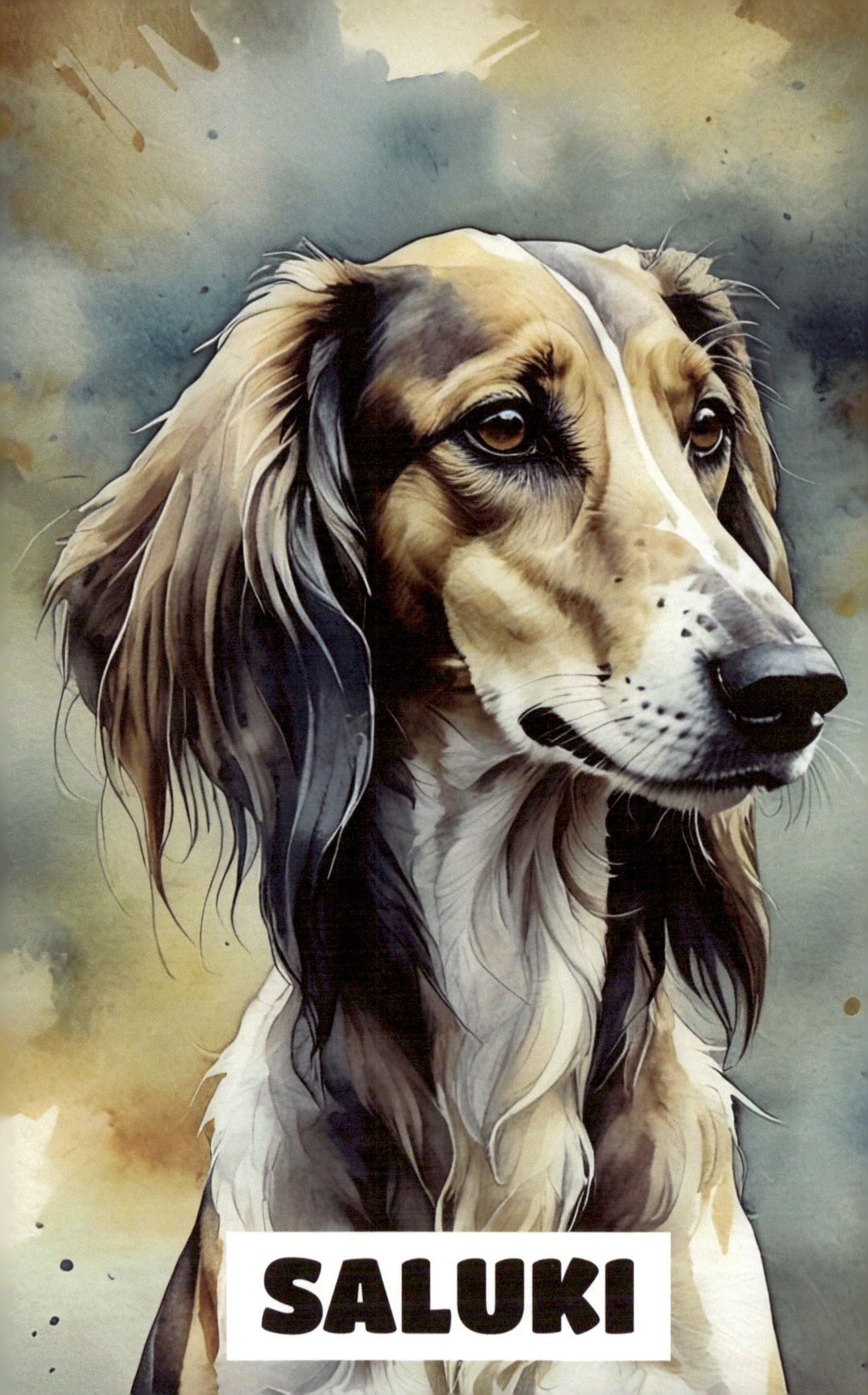

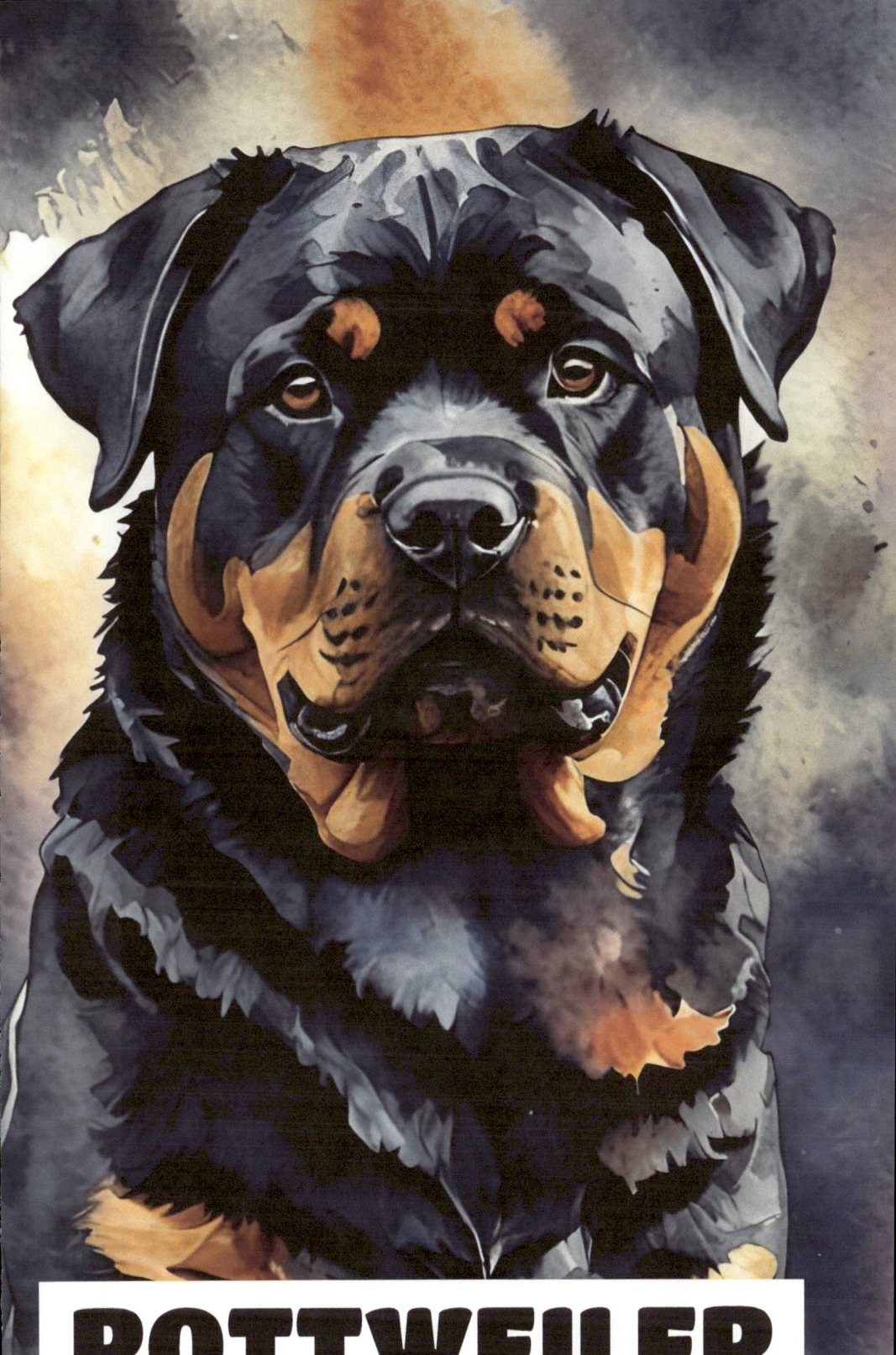

ROTTWEILER

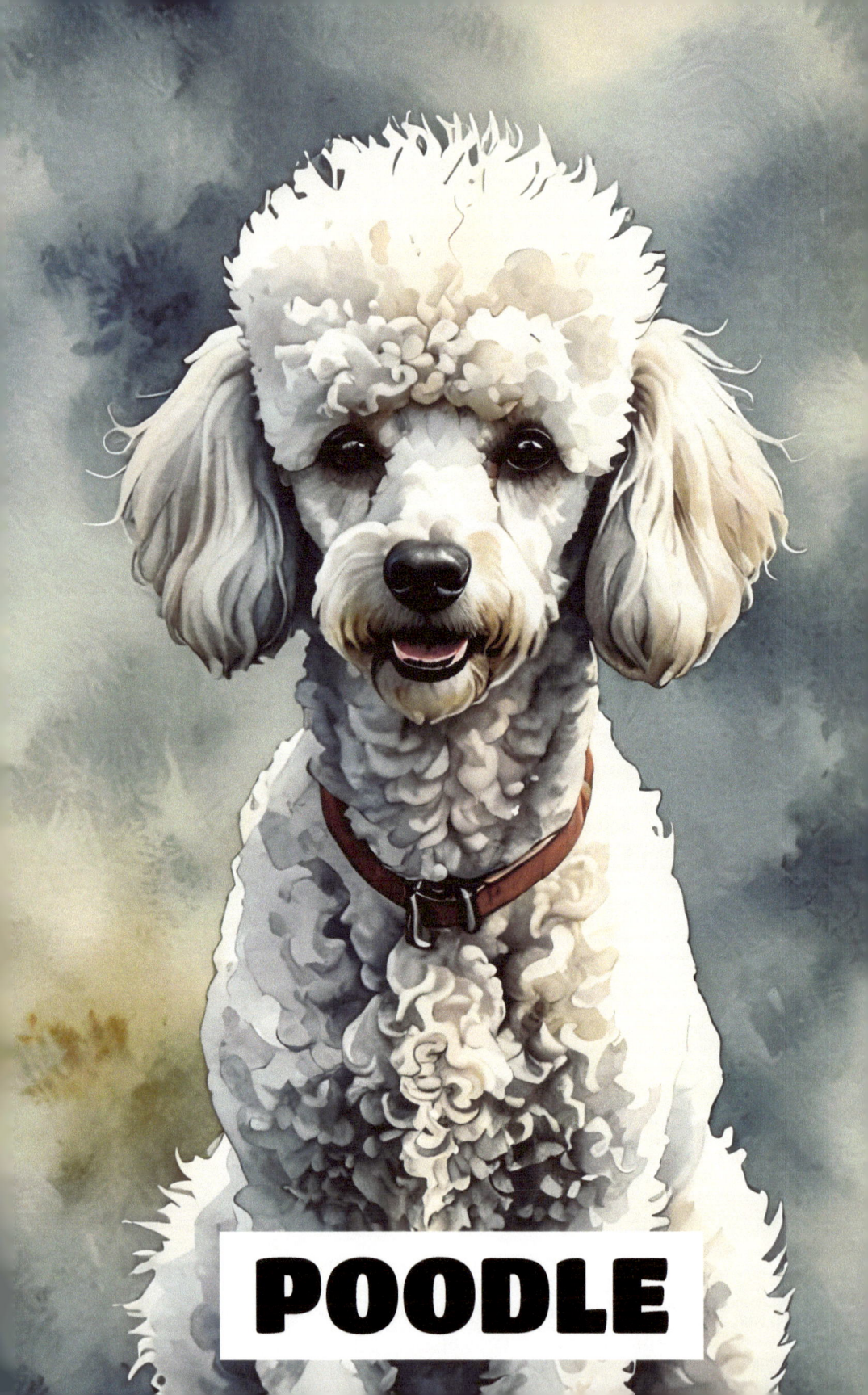

POODLE

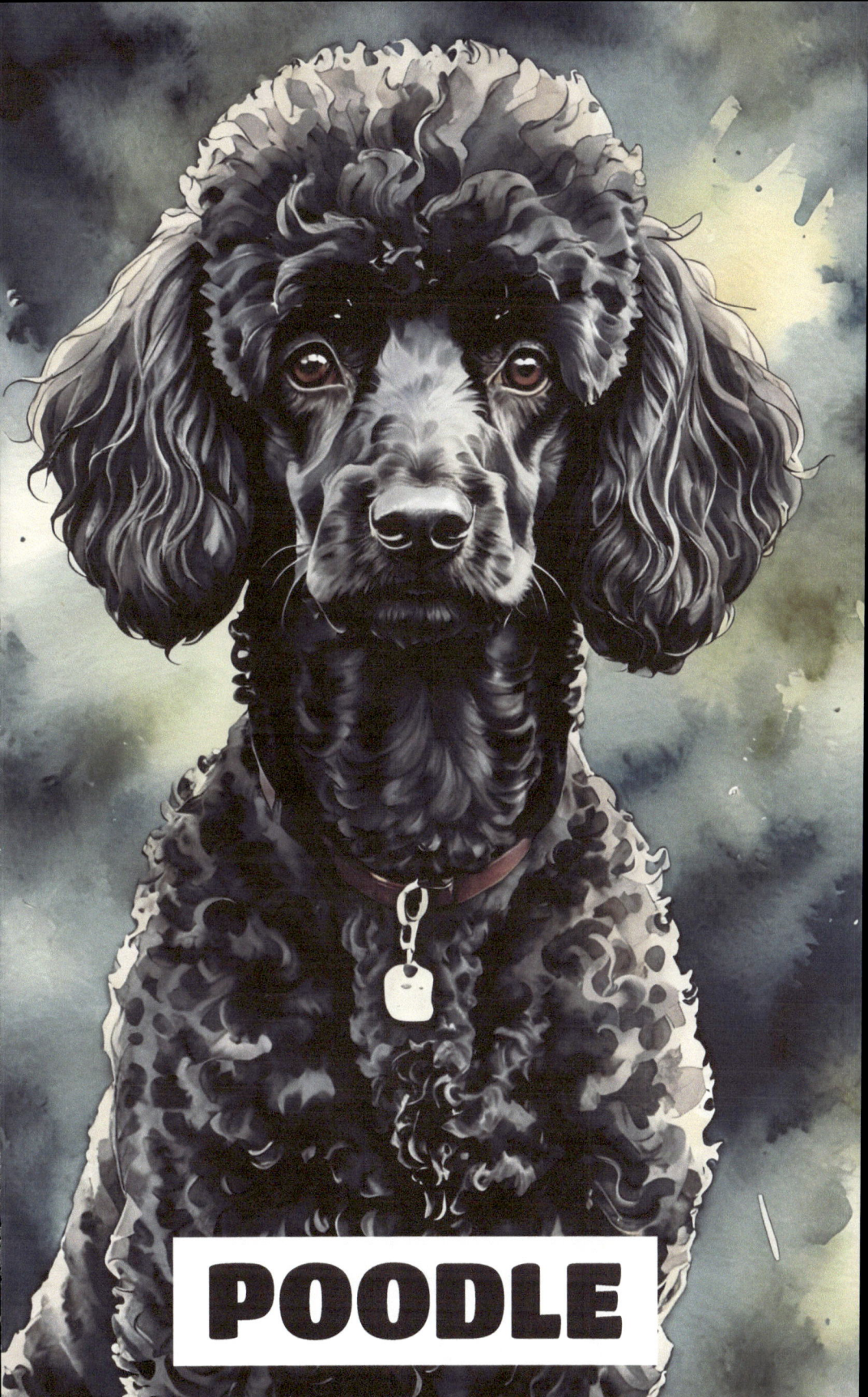

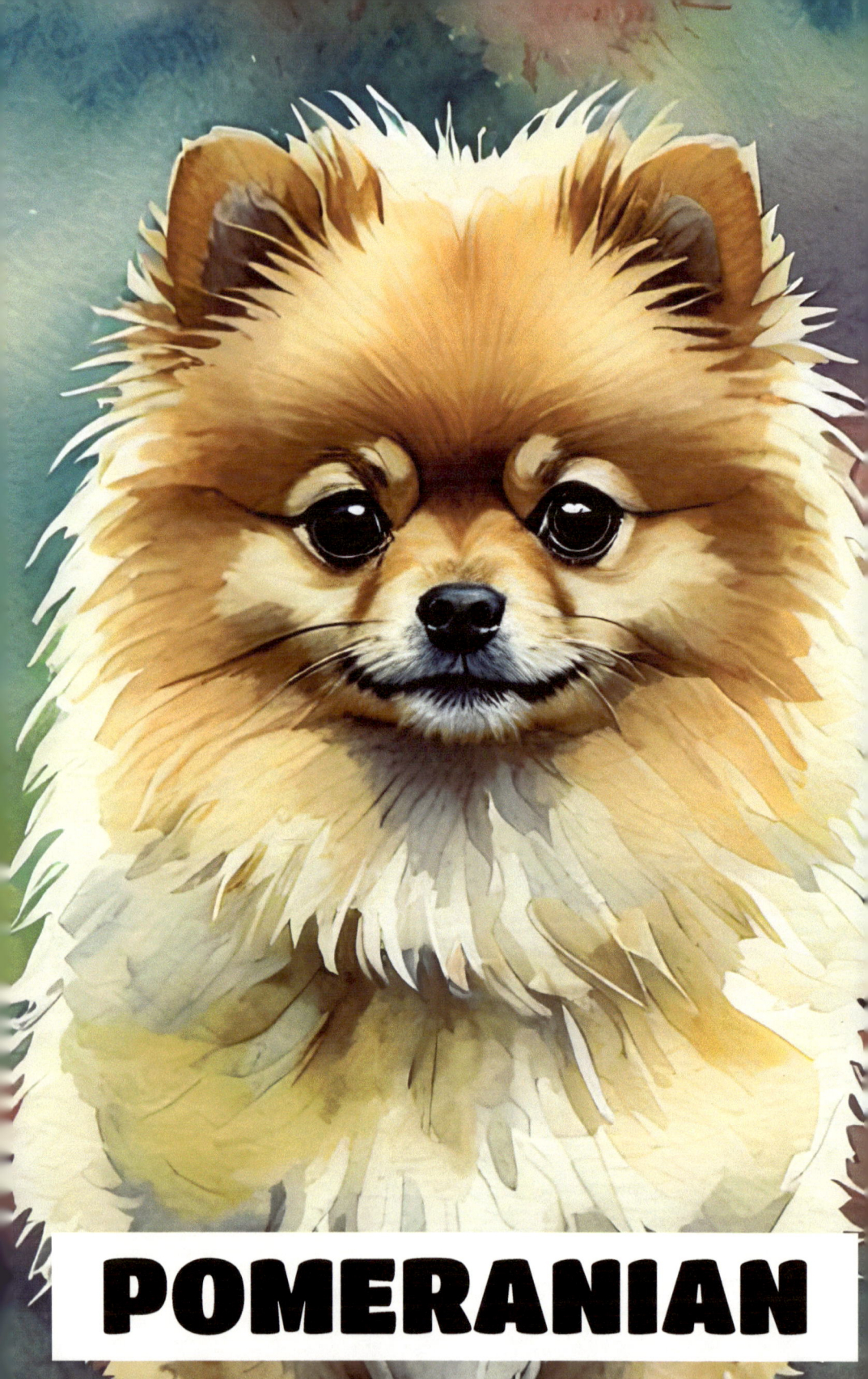

POMERANIAN

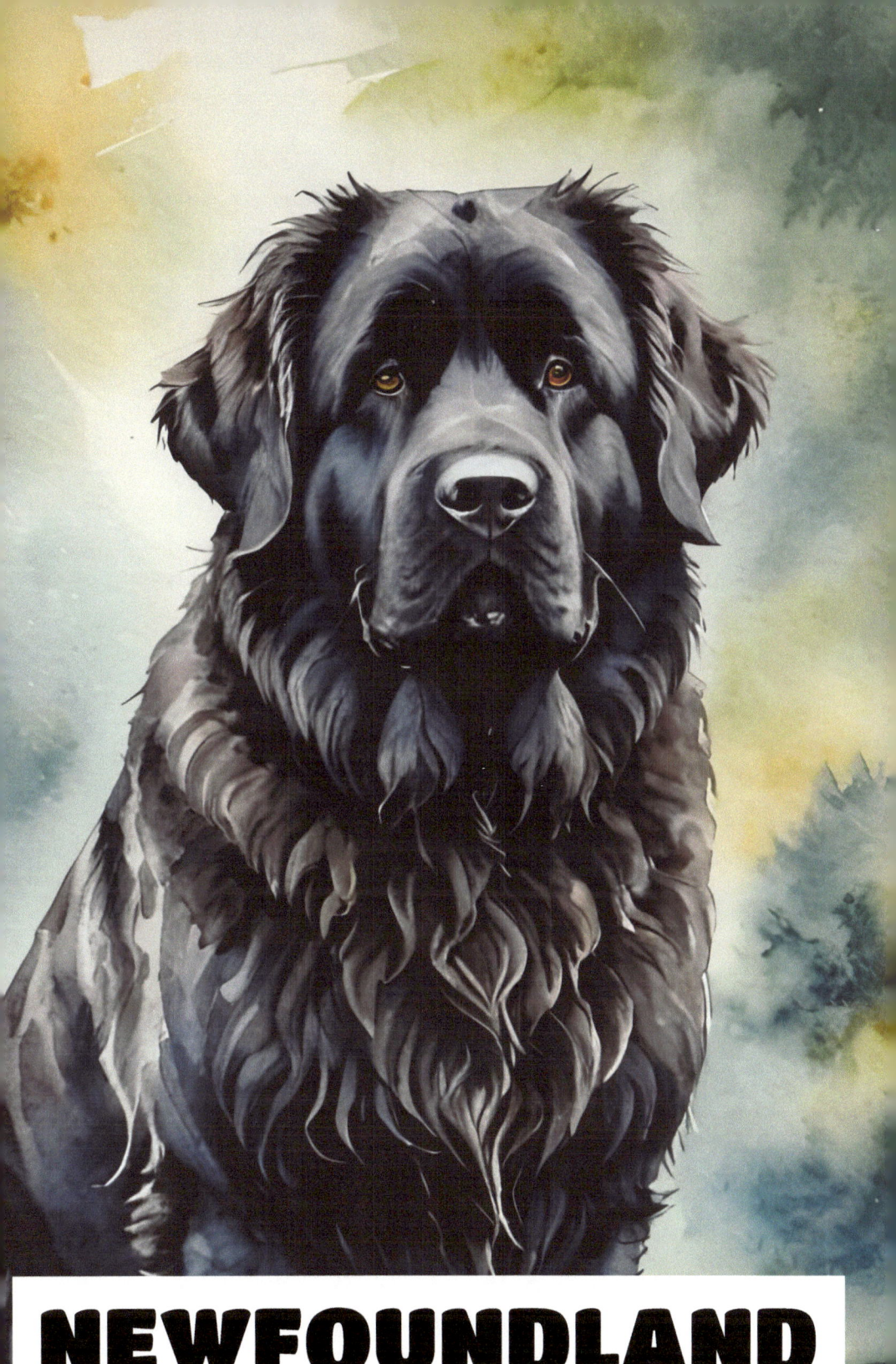

NEWFOUNDLAND

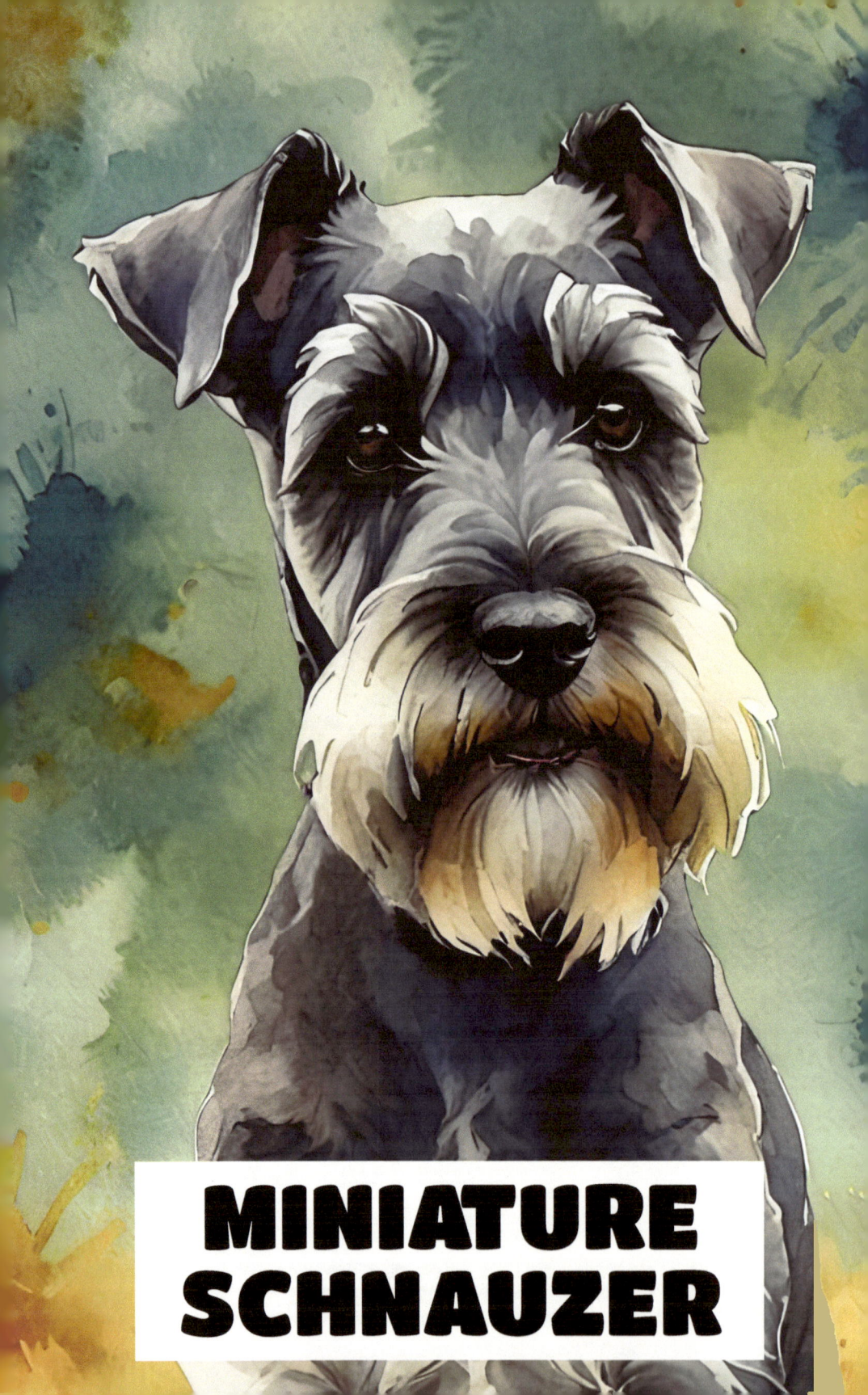

MINIATURE SCHNAUZER

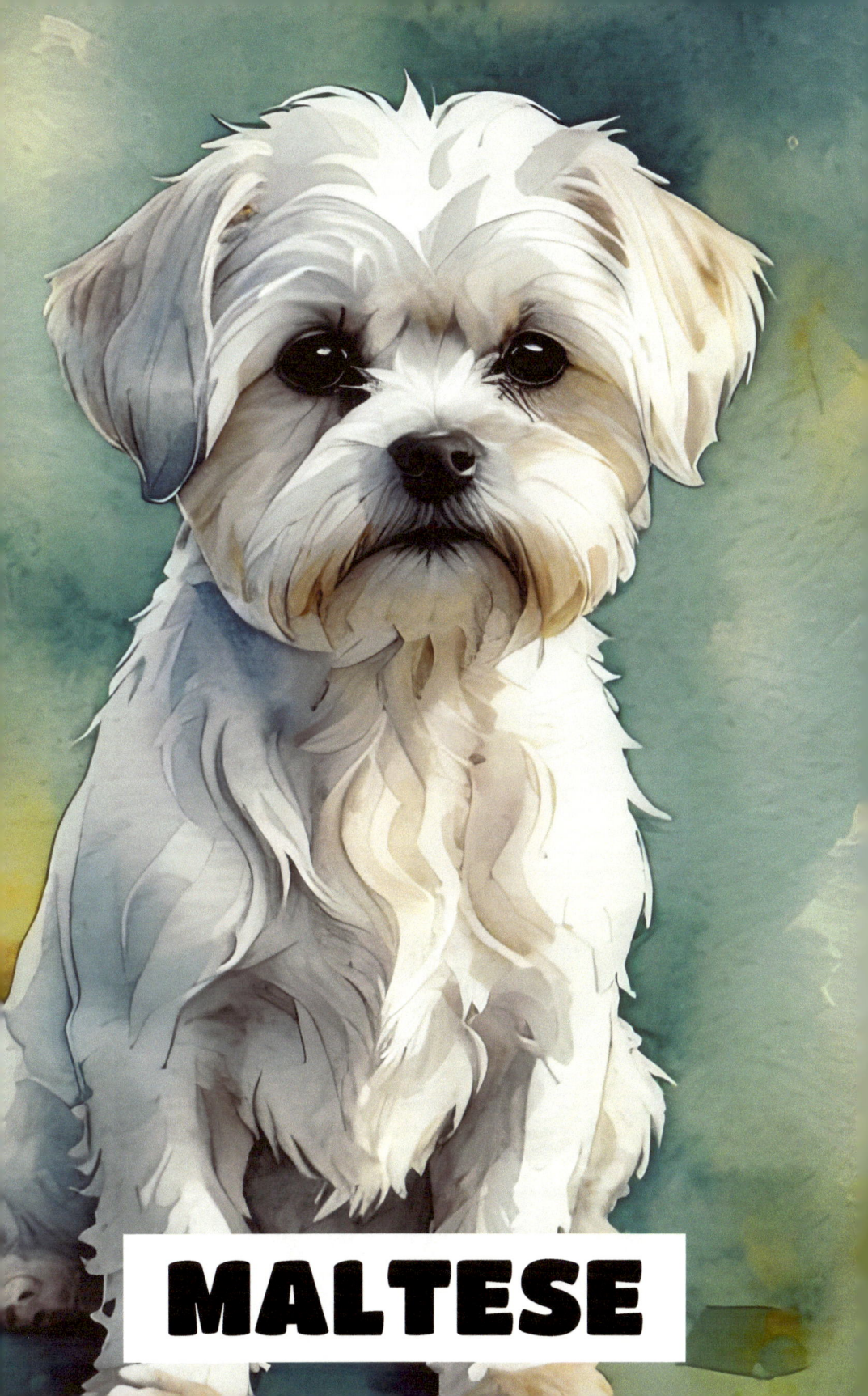

MALTESE

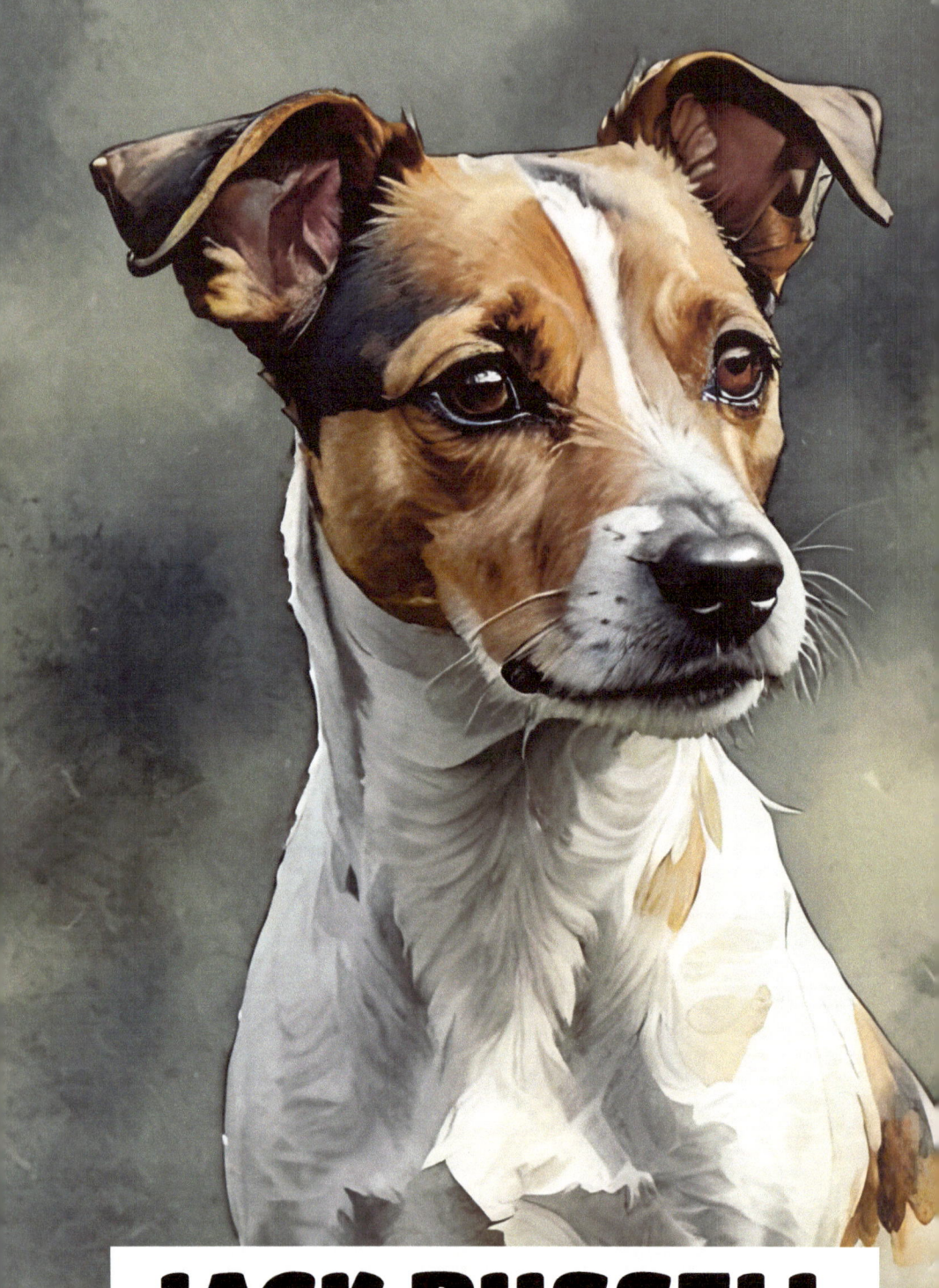

JACK RUSSELL TERRIER

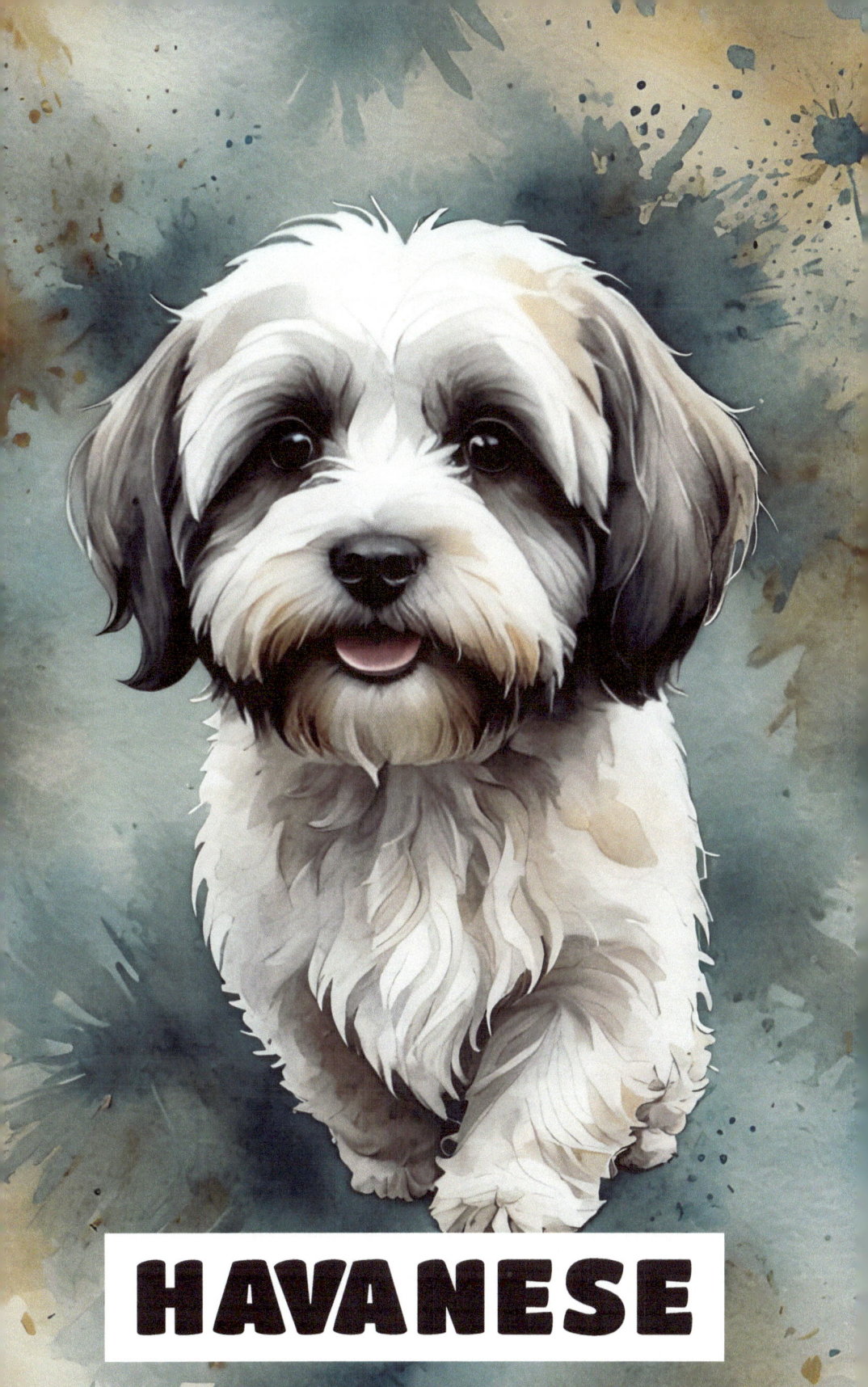

HAVANESE

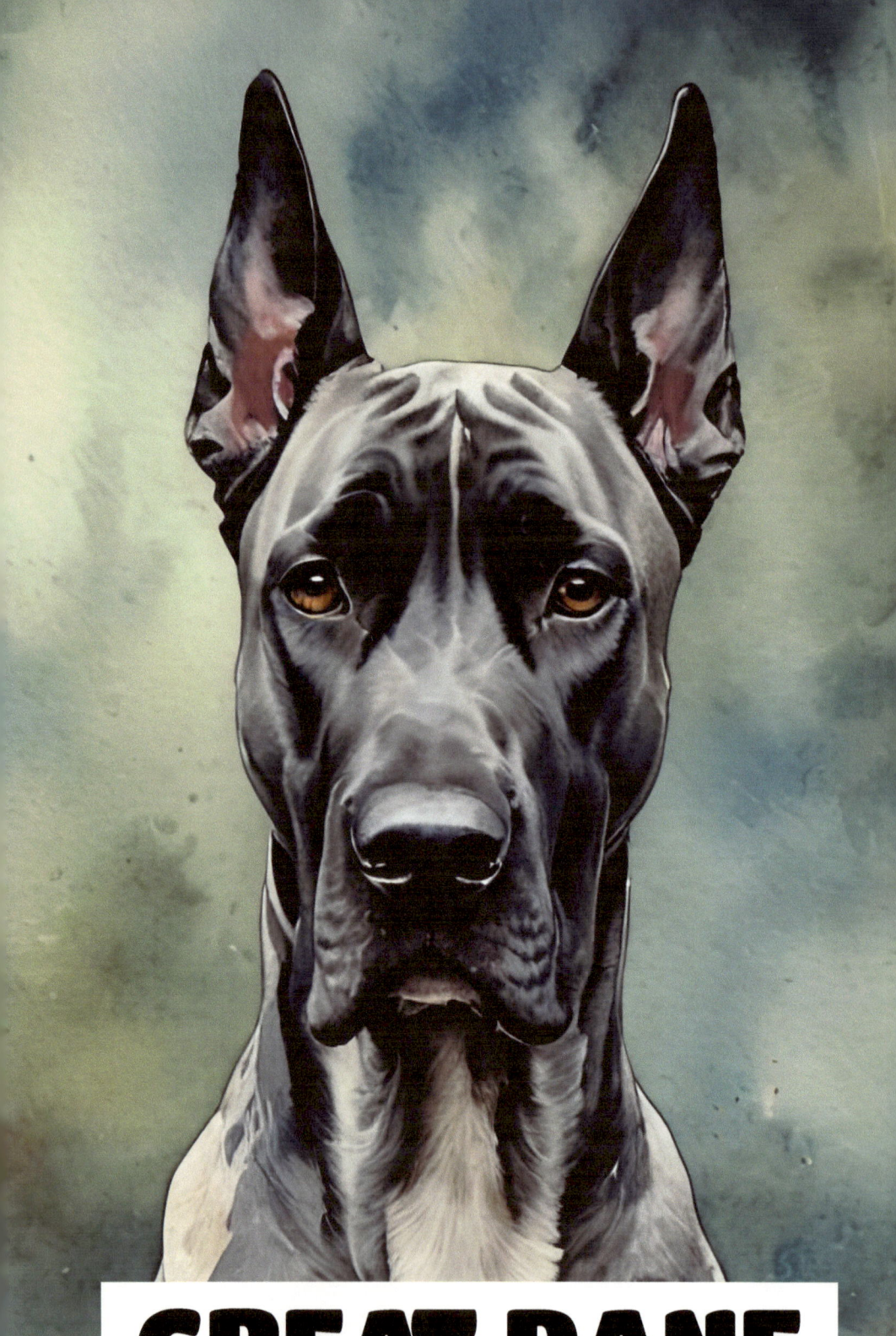

GREAT DANE

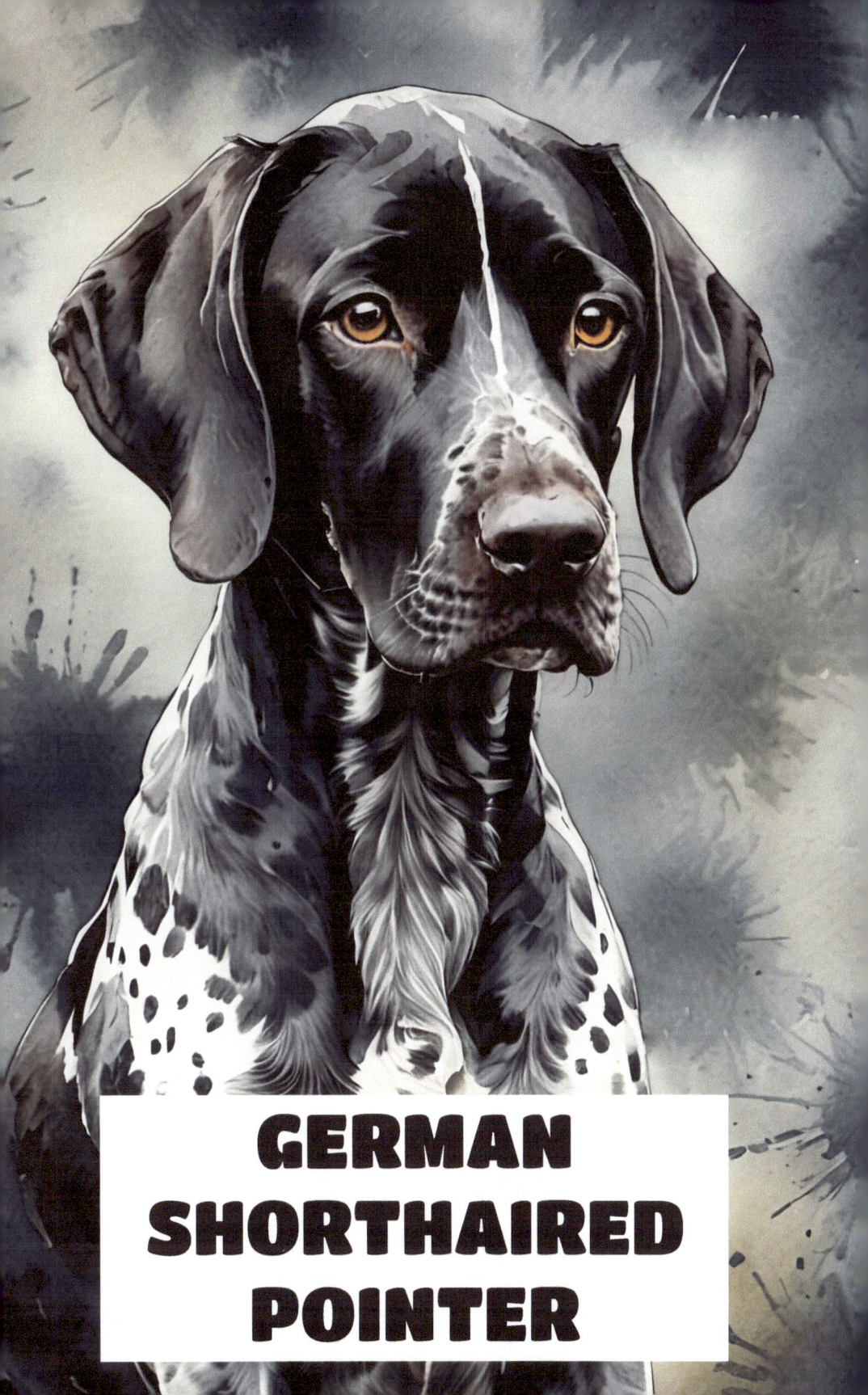

GERMAN SHORTHAIRED POINTER

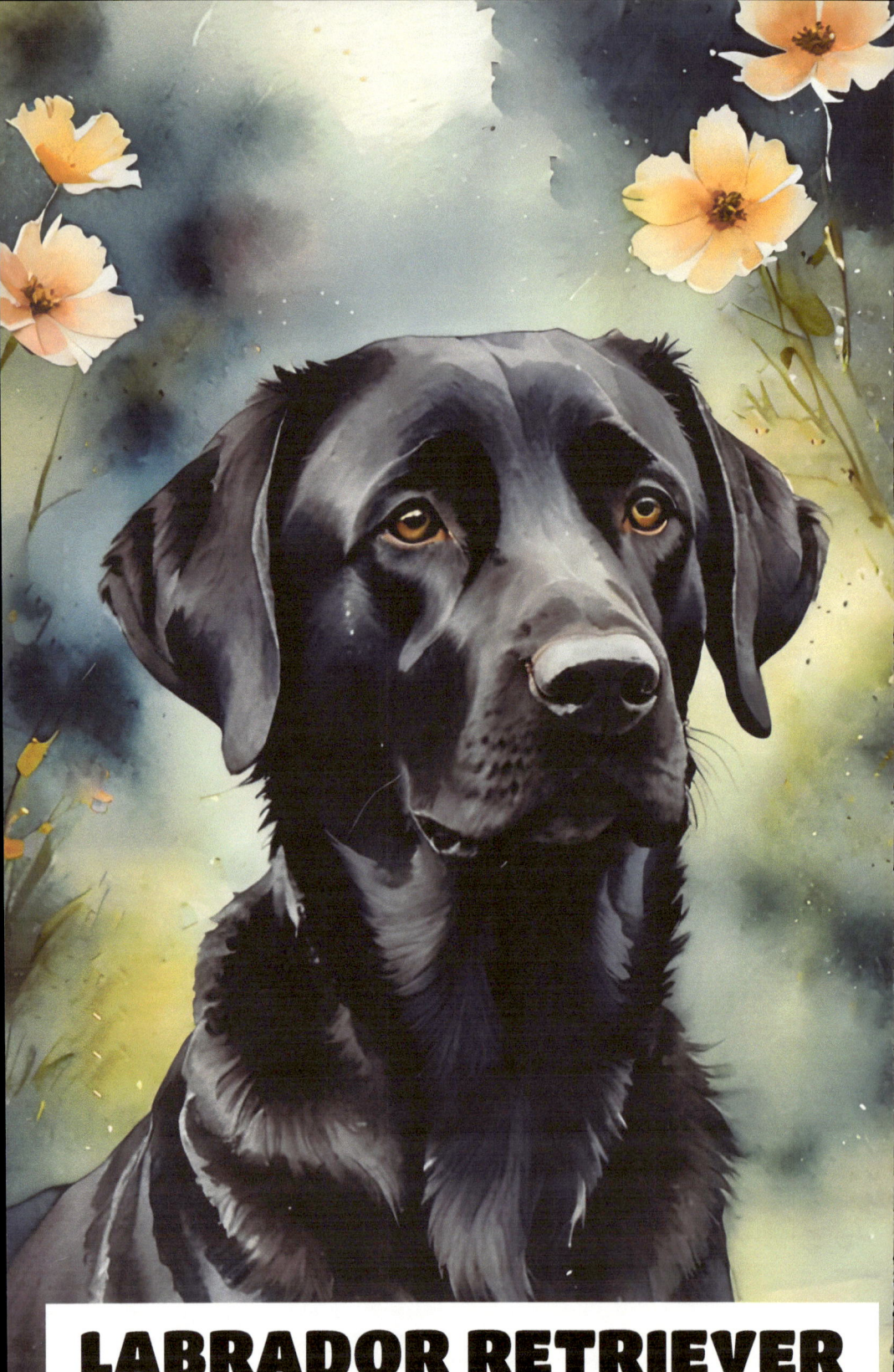

LABRADOR RETRIEVER

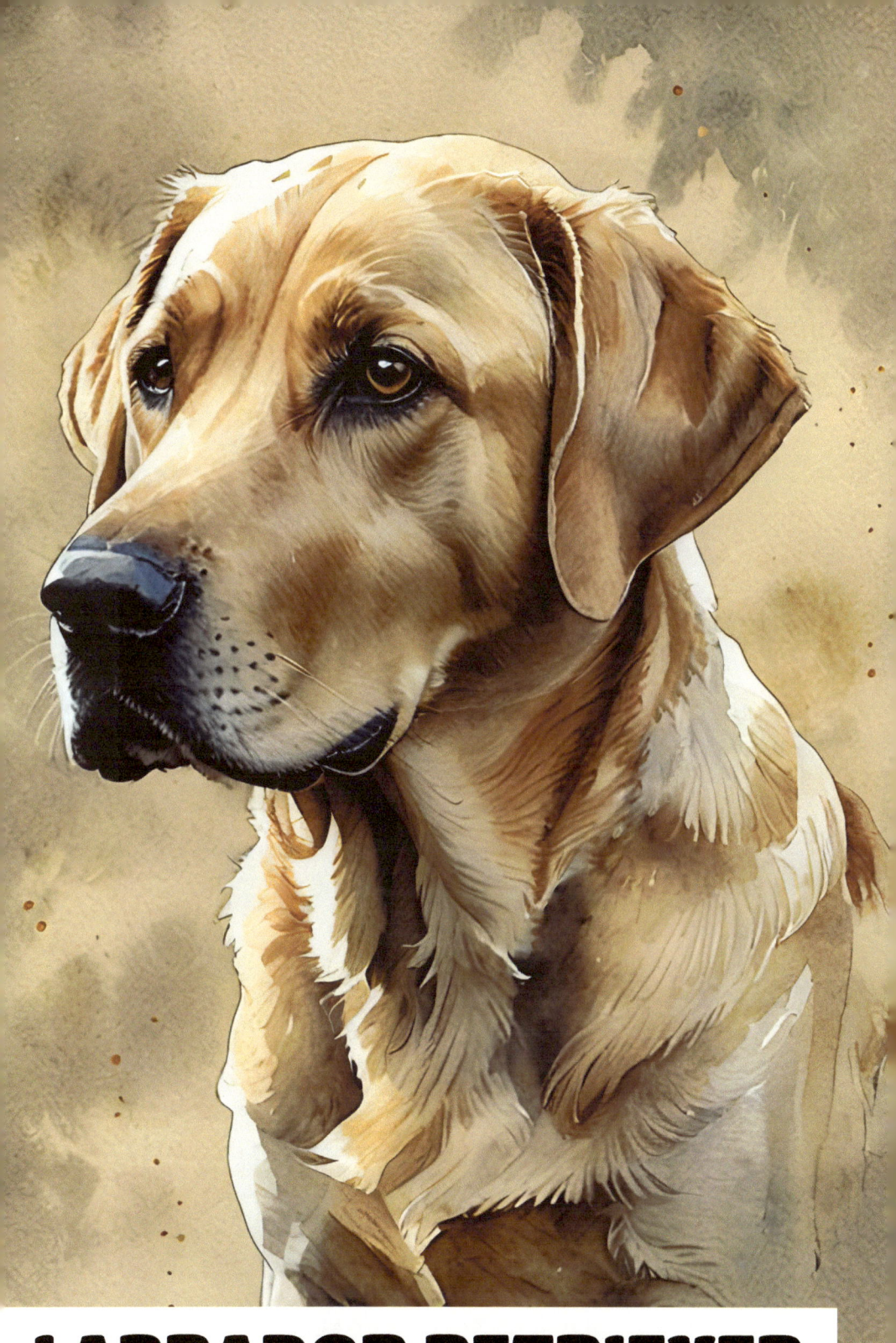

LABRADOR RETRIEVER

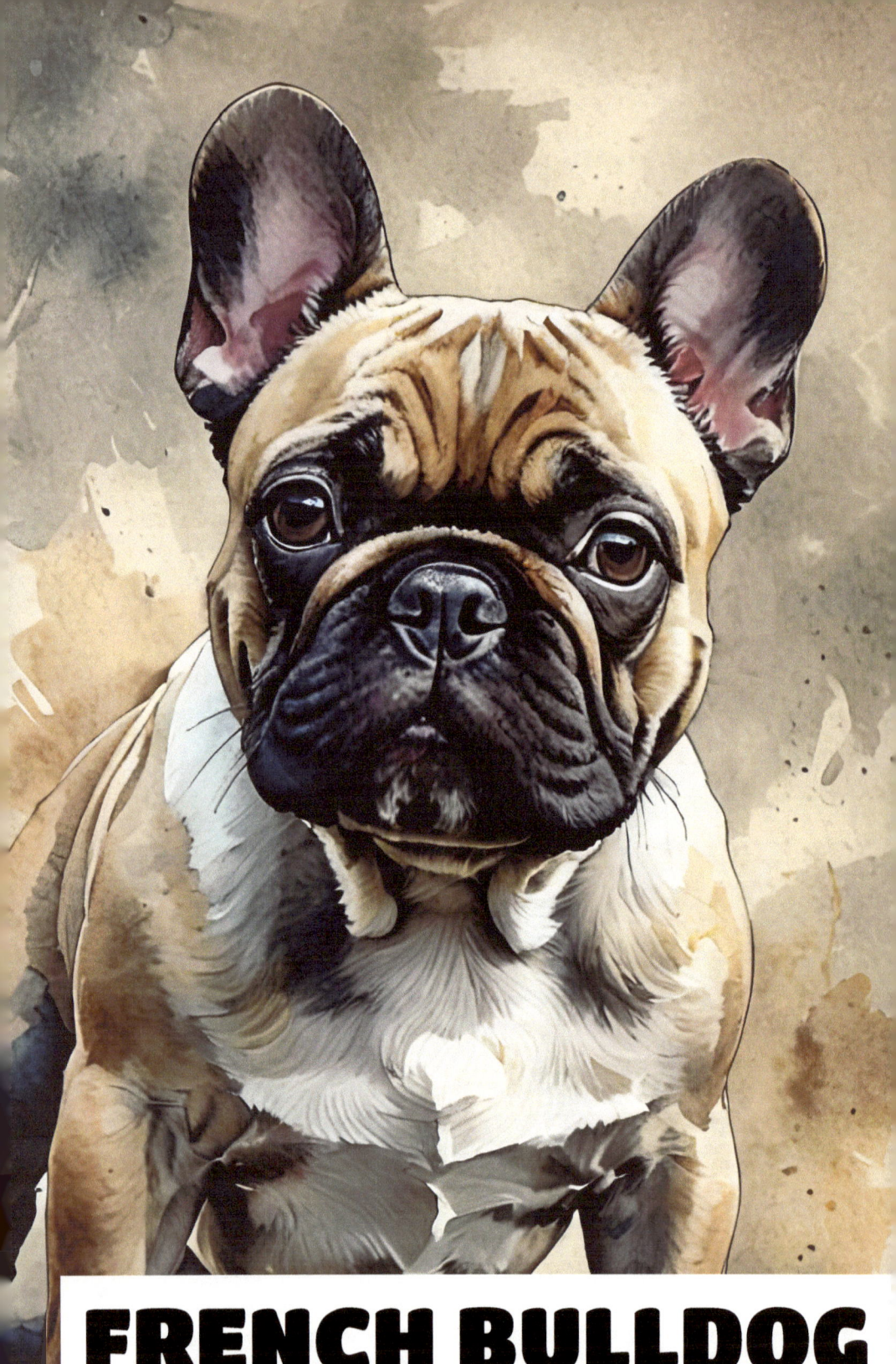

FRENCH BULLDOG

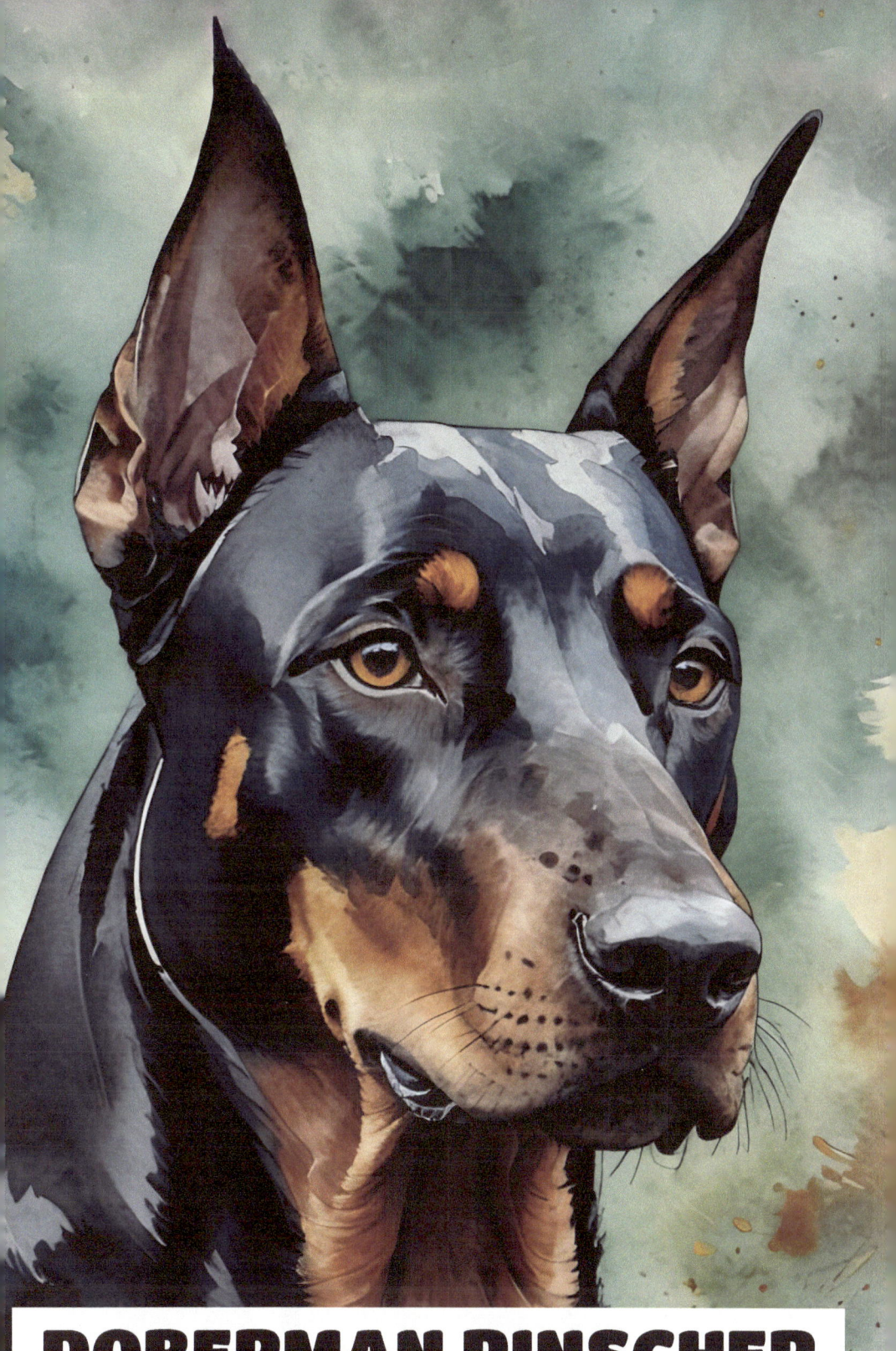

DOBERMAN PINSCHER

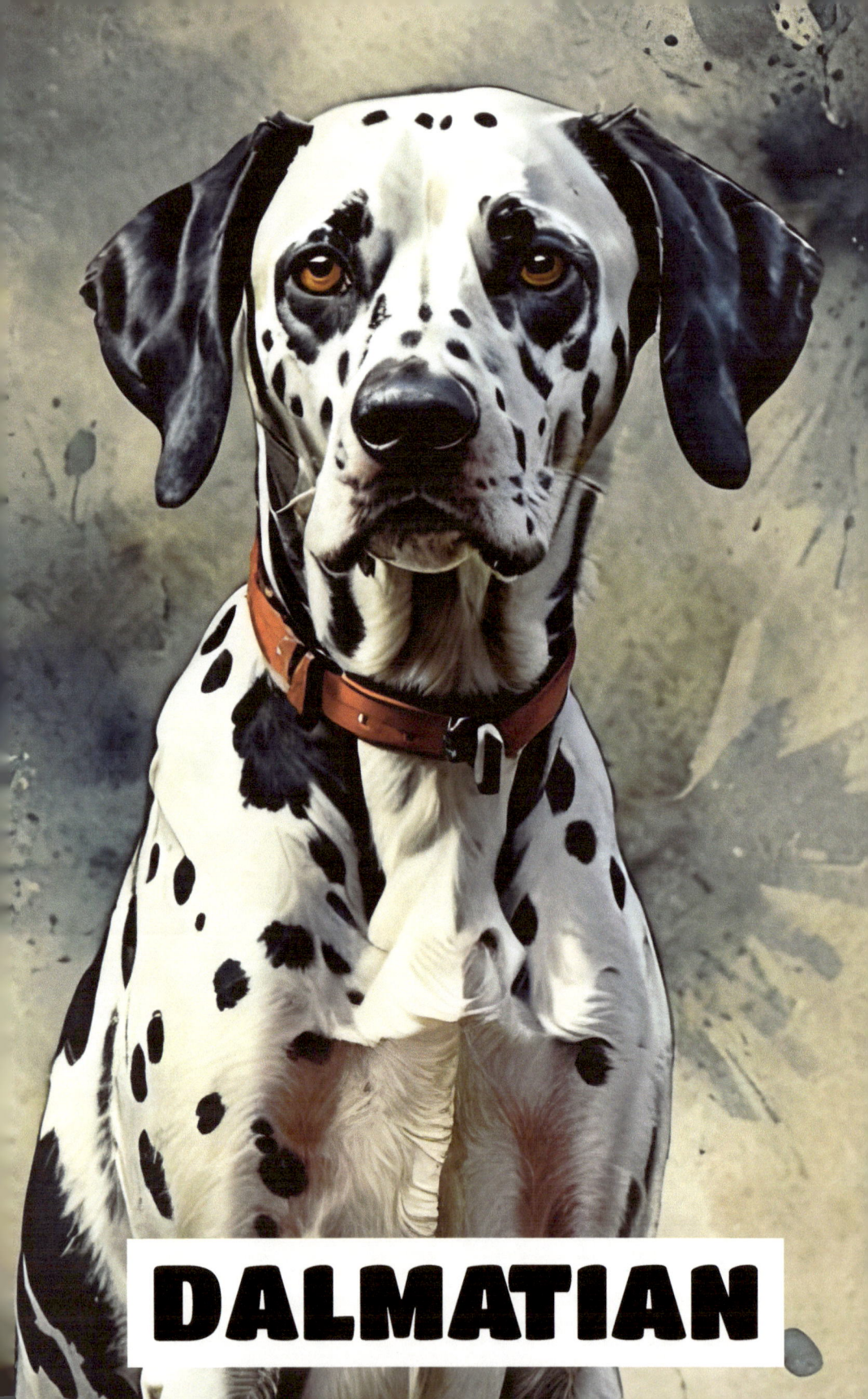

DALMATIAN

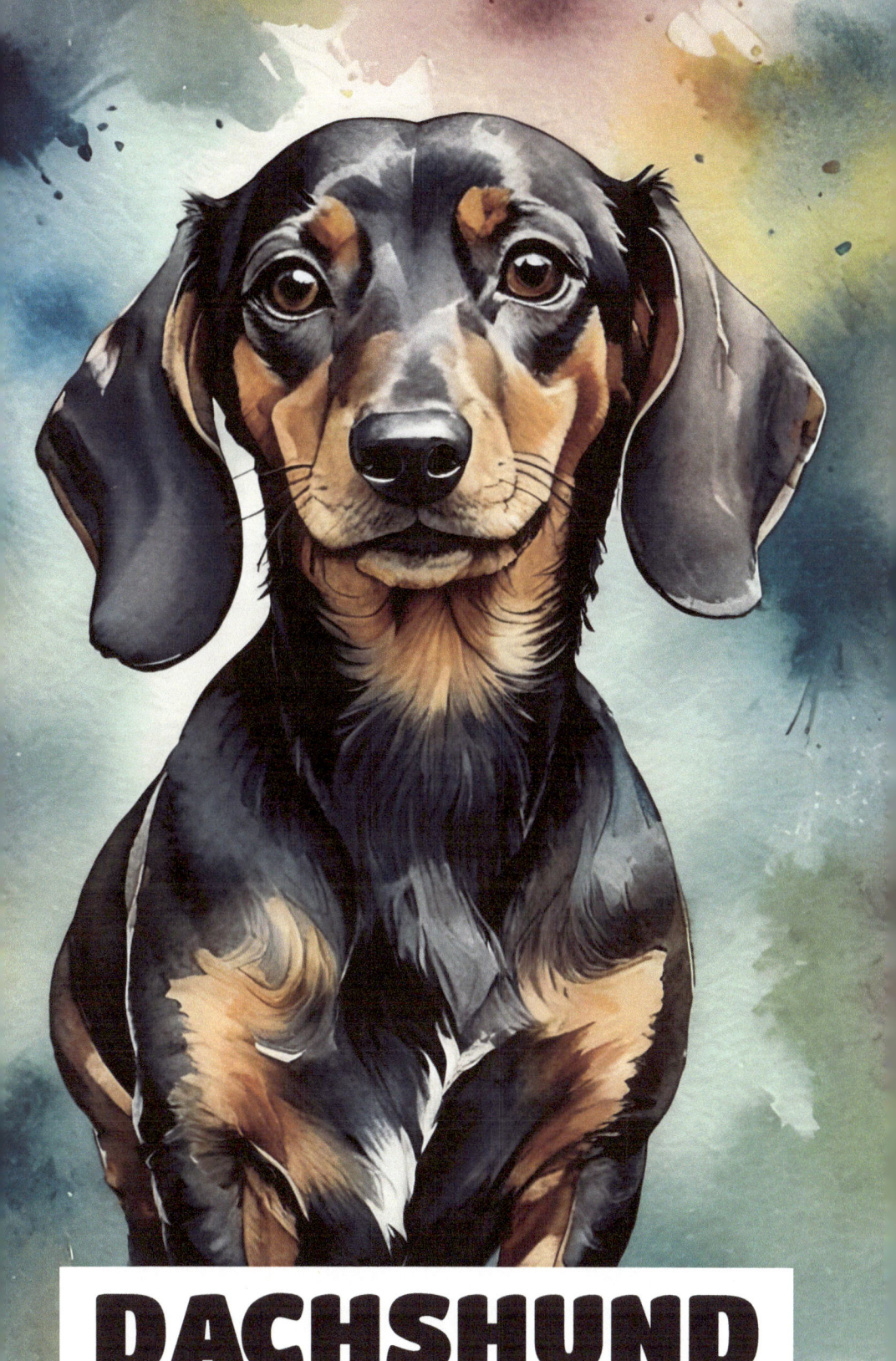

DACHSHUND

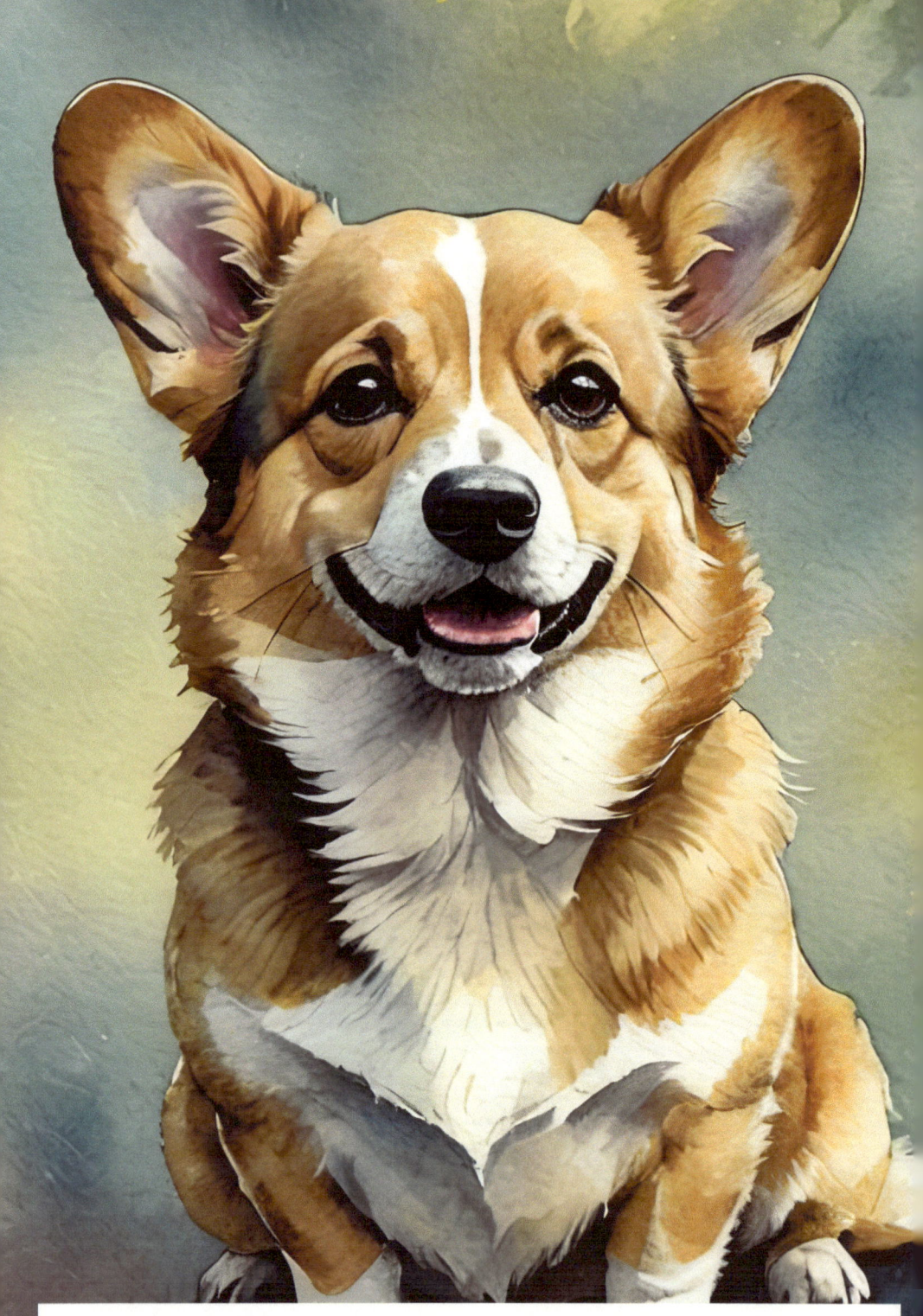

WELSH CORGI

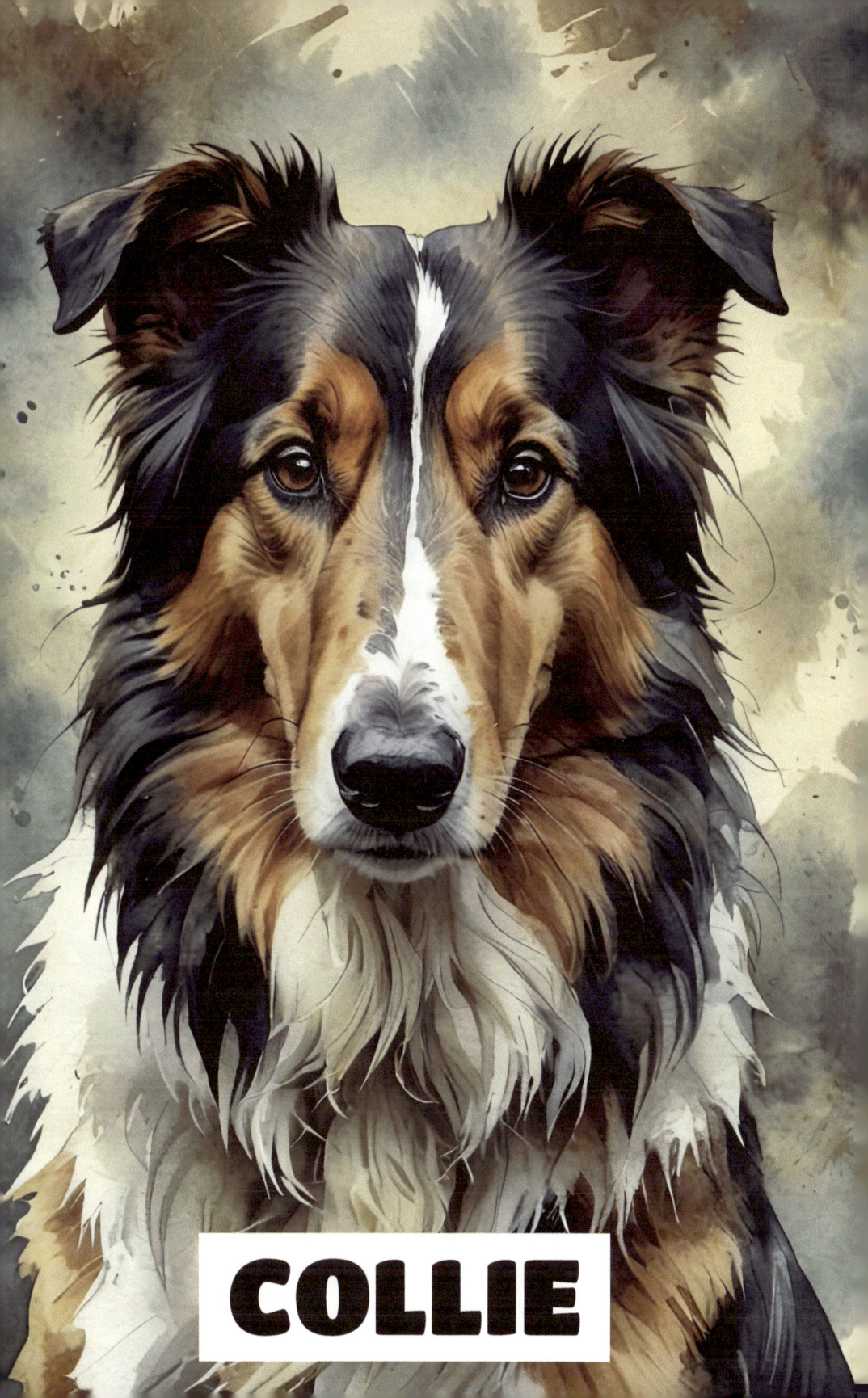

COLLIE

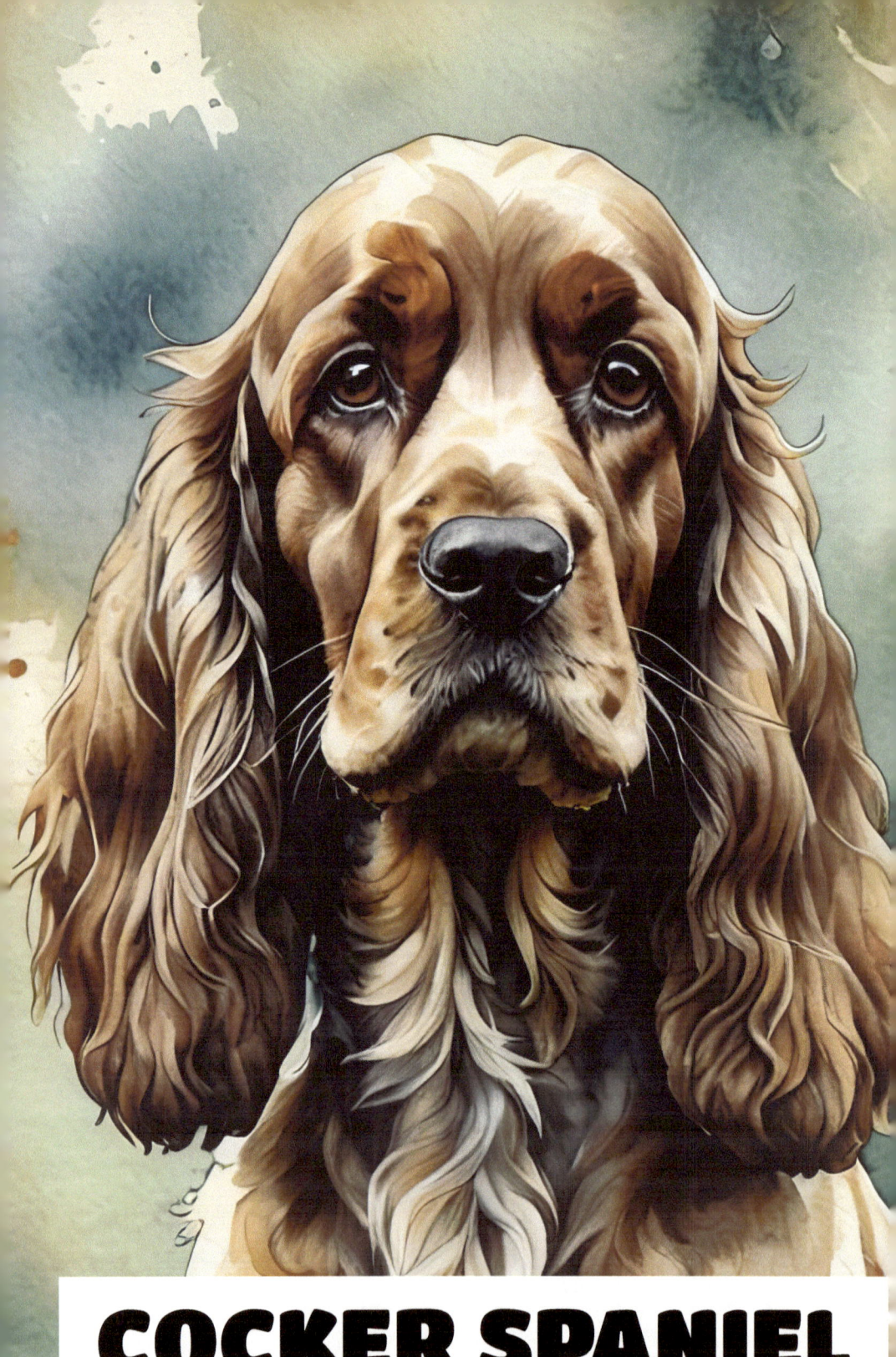

COCKER SPANIEL

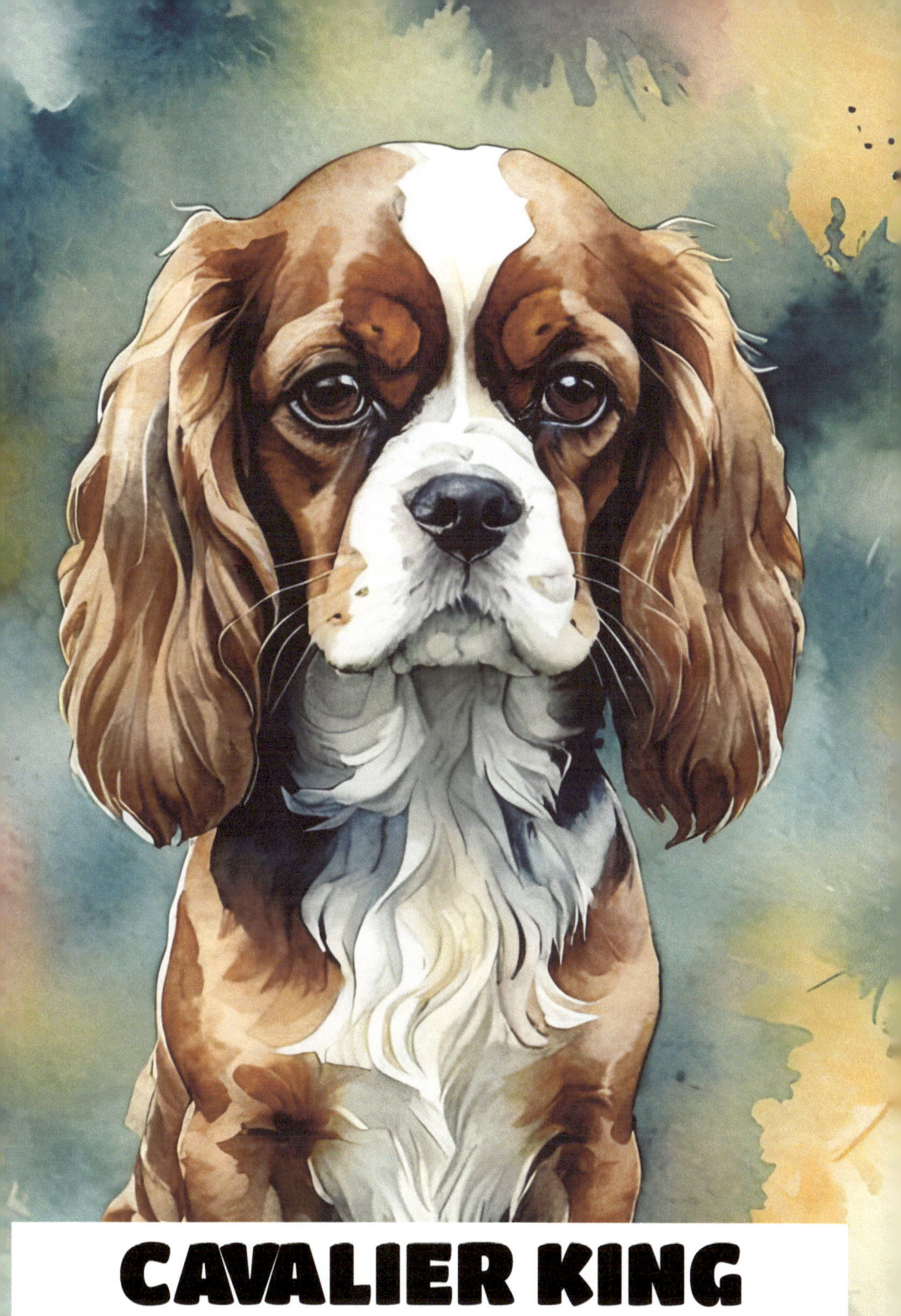

CAVALIER KING CHARLES SPANIEL

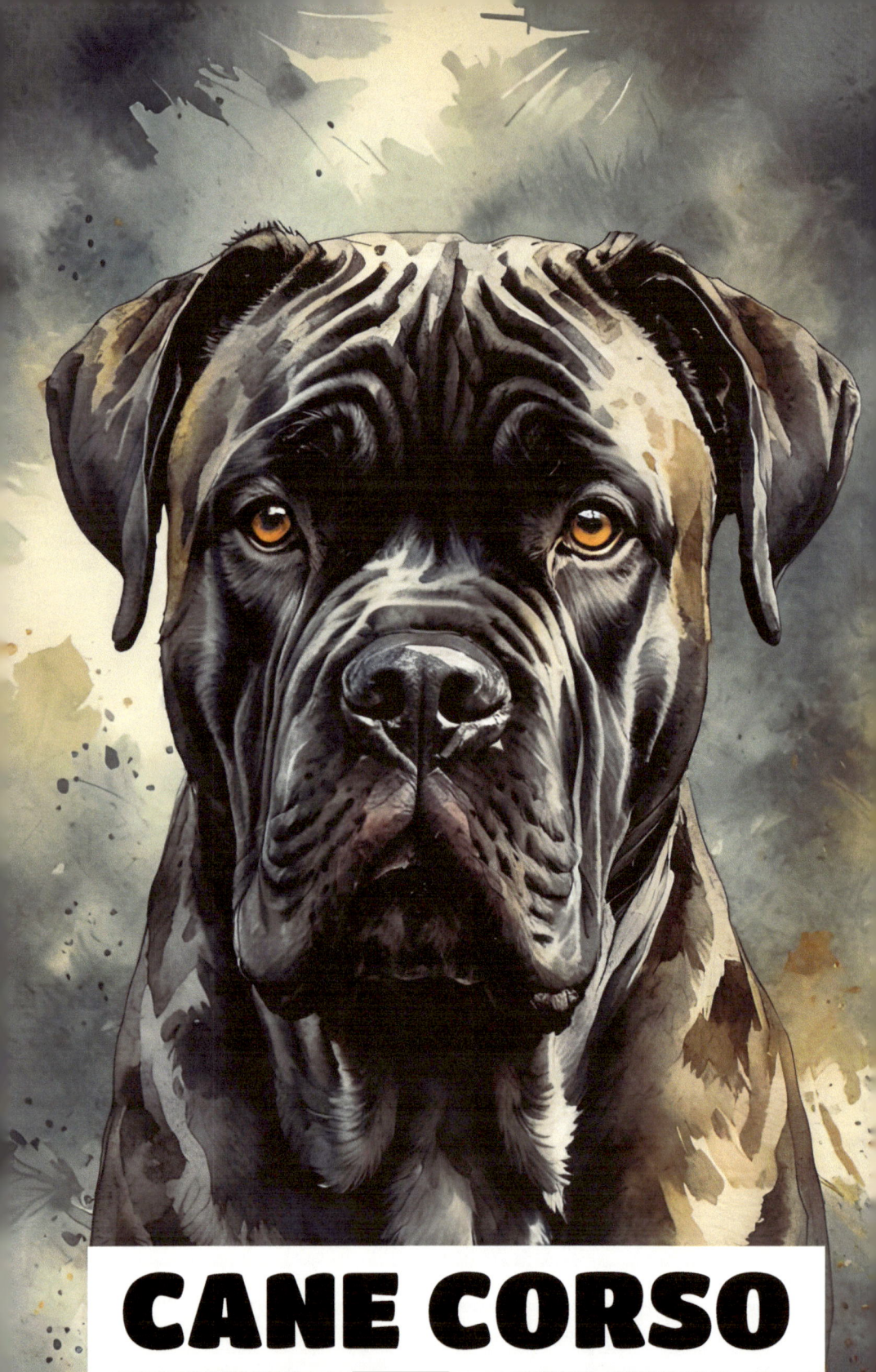

CANE CORSO

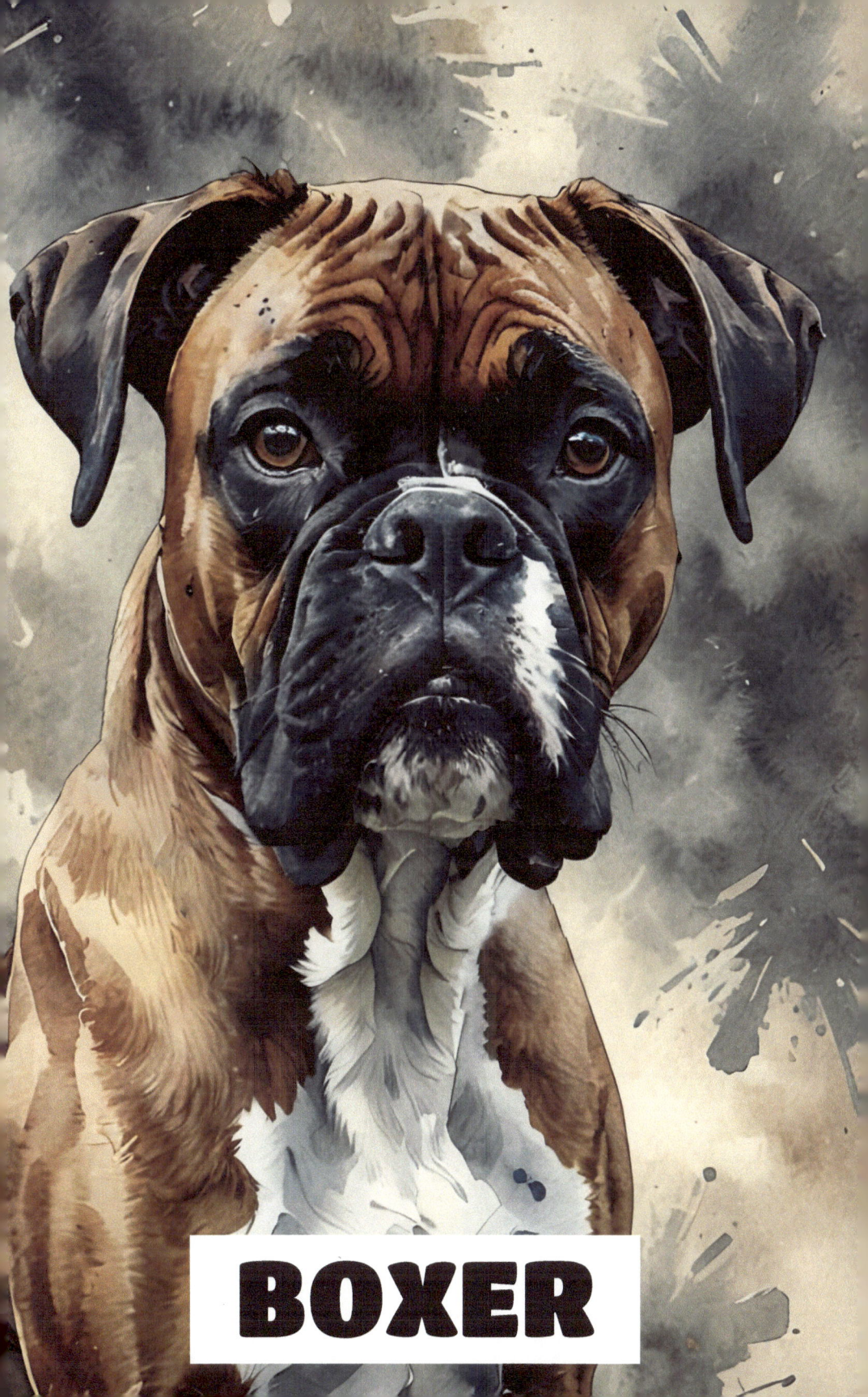

BOXER

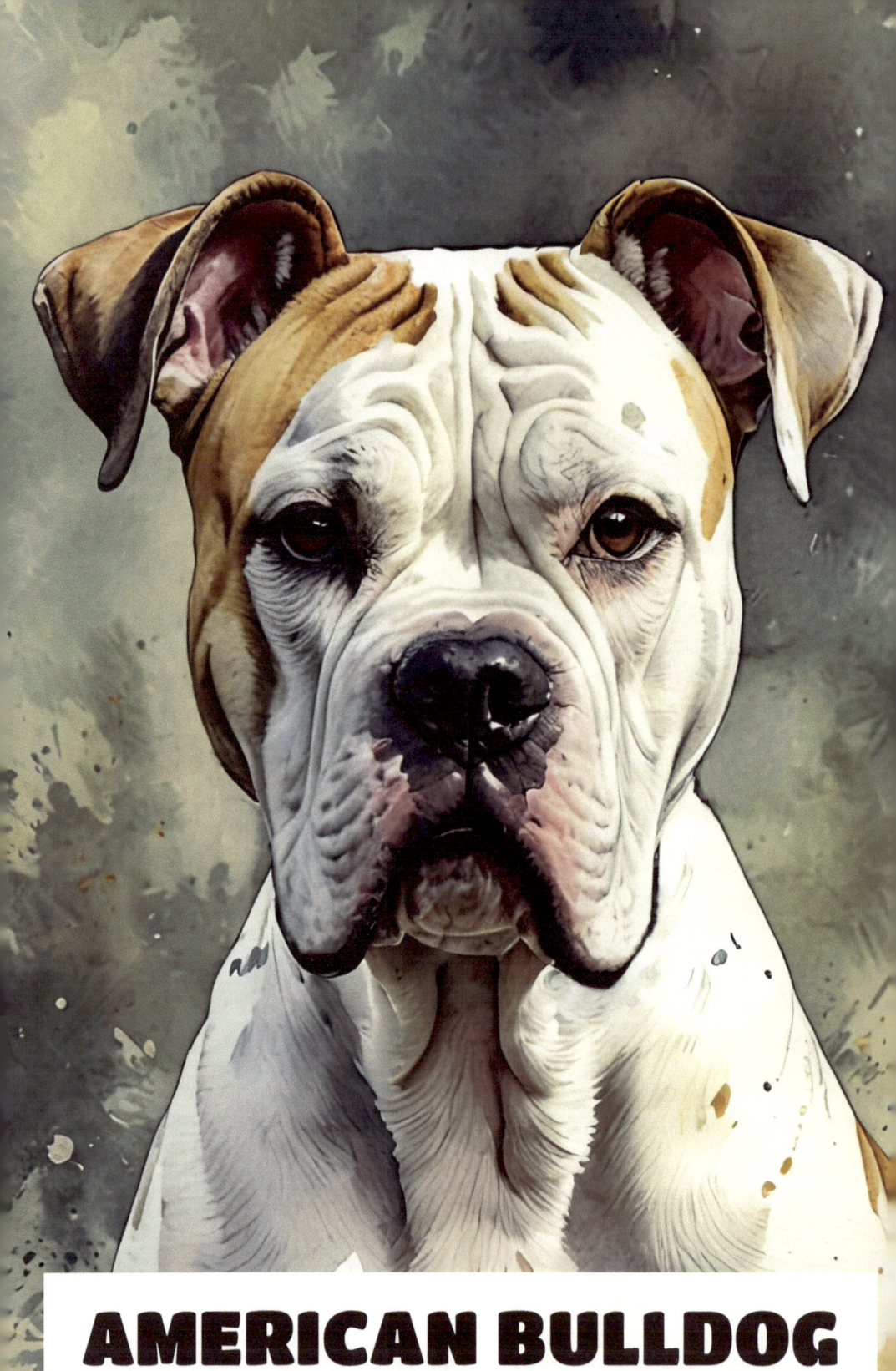

AMERICAN BULLDOG

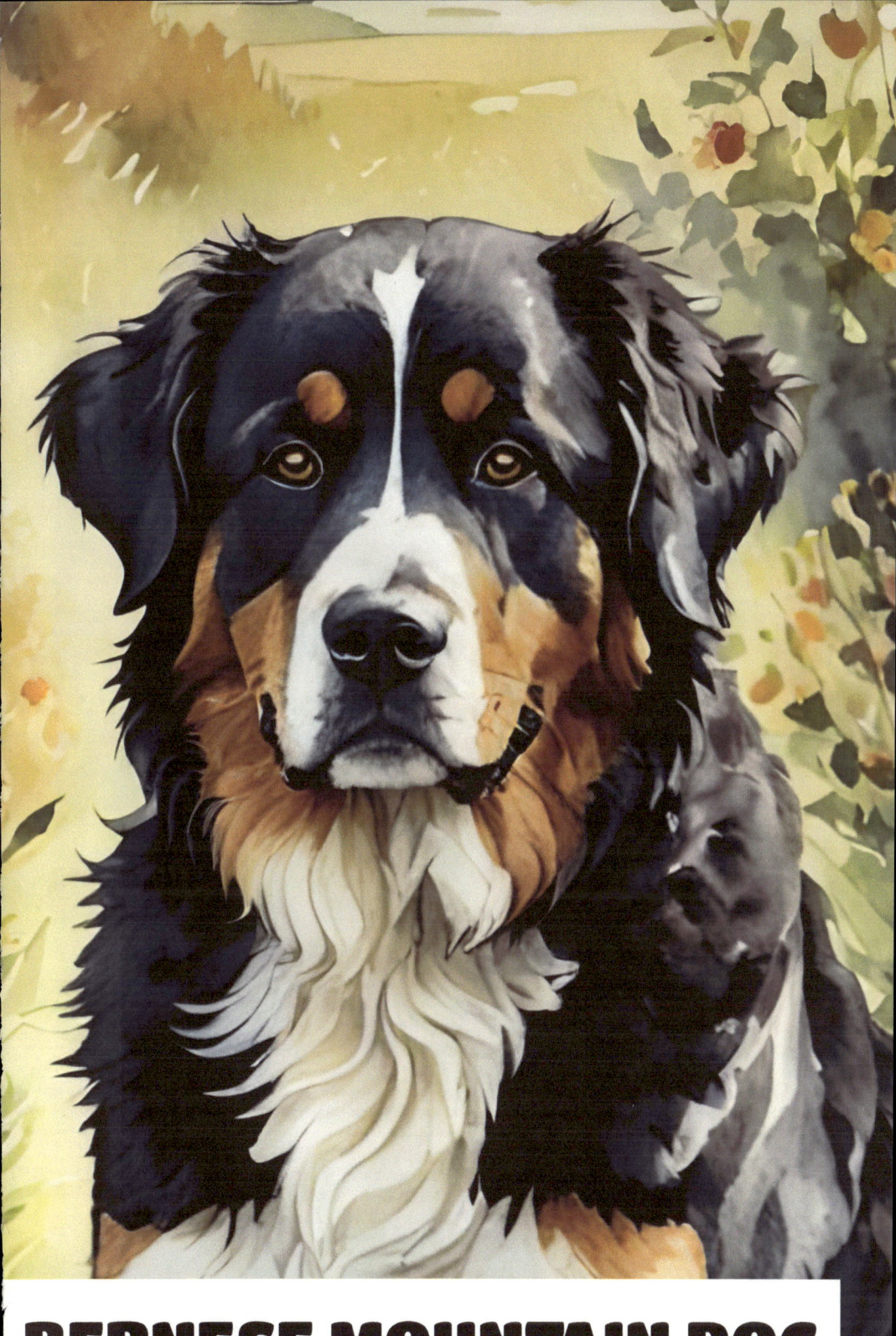

BERNESE MOUNTAIN DOG

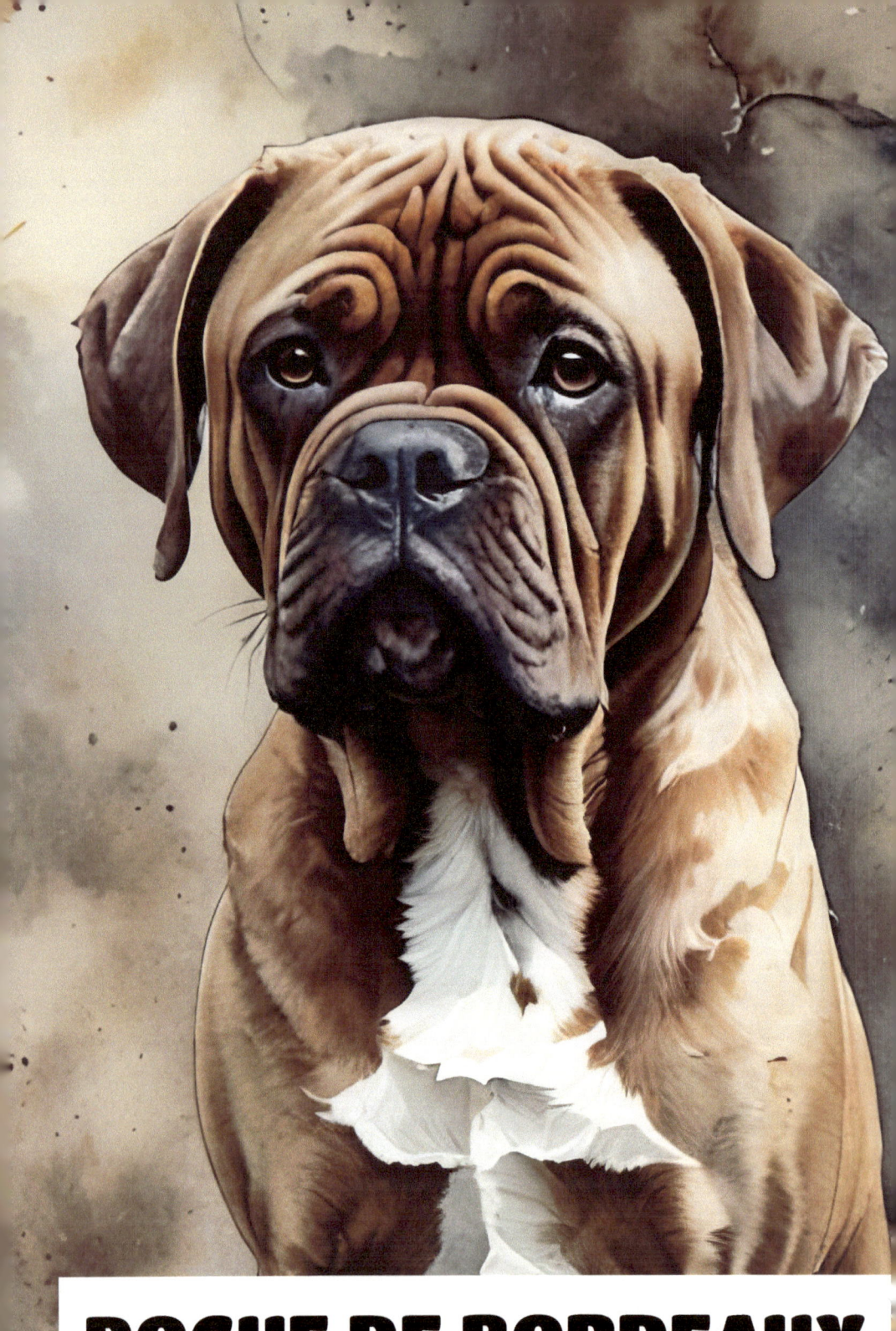

DOGUE DE BORDEAUX

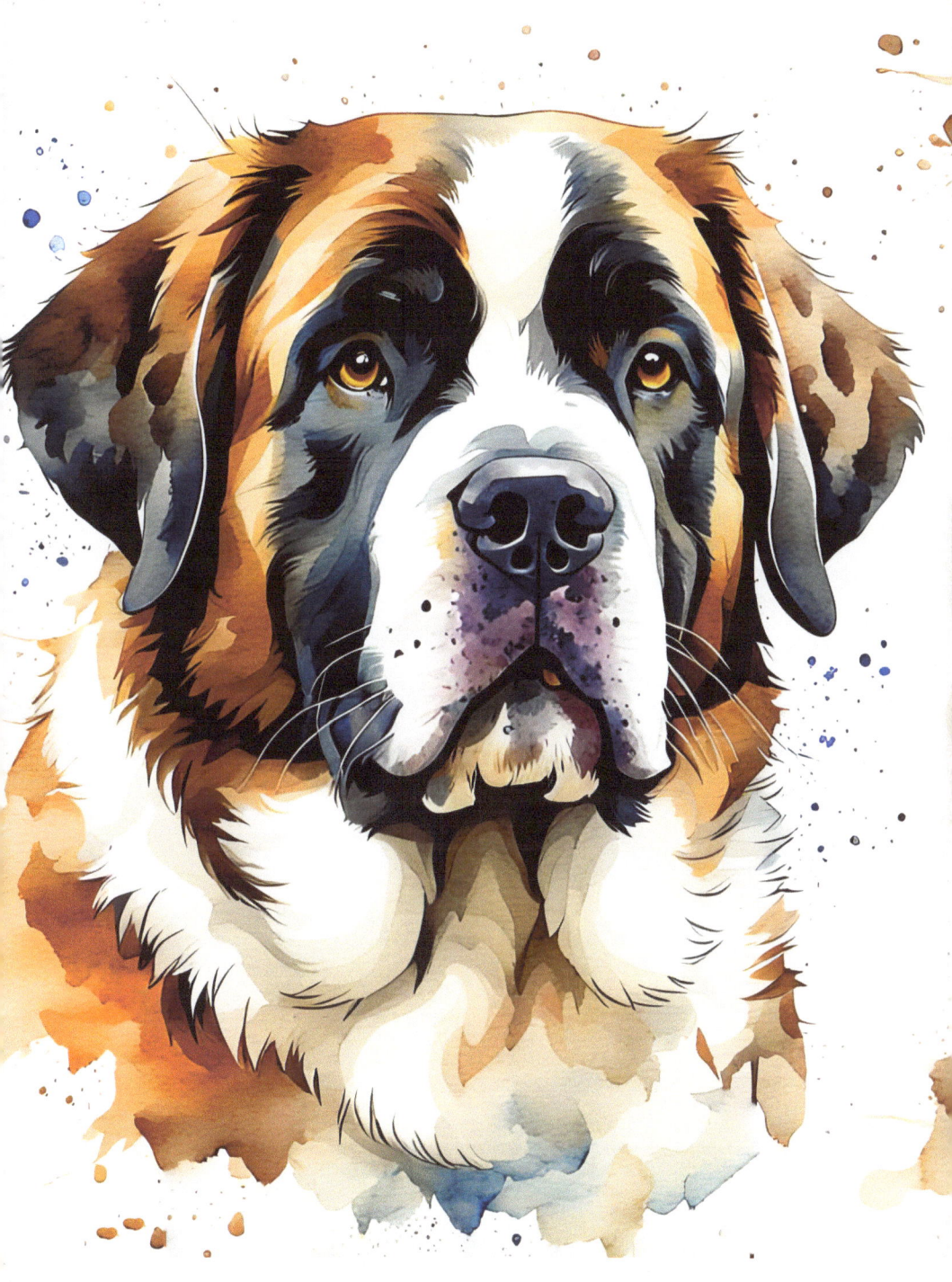

SAINT BERNARD

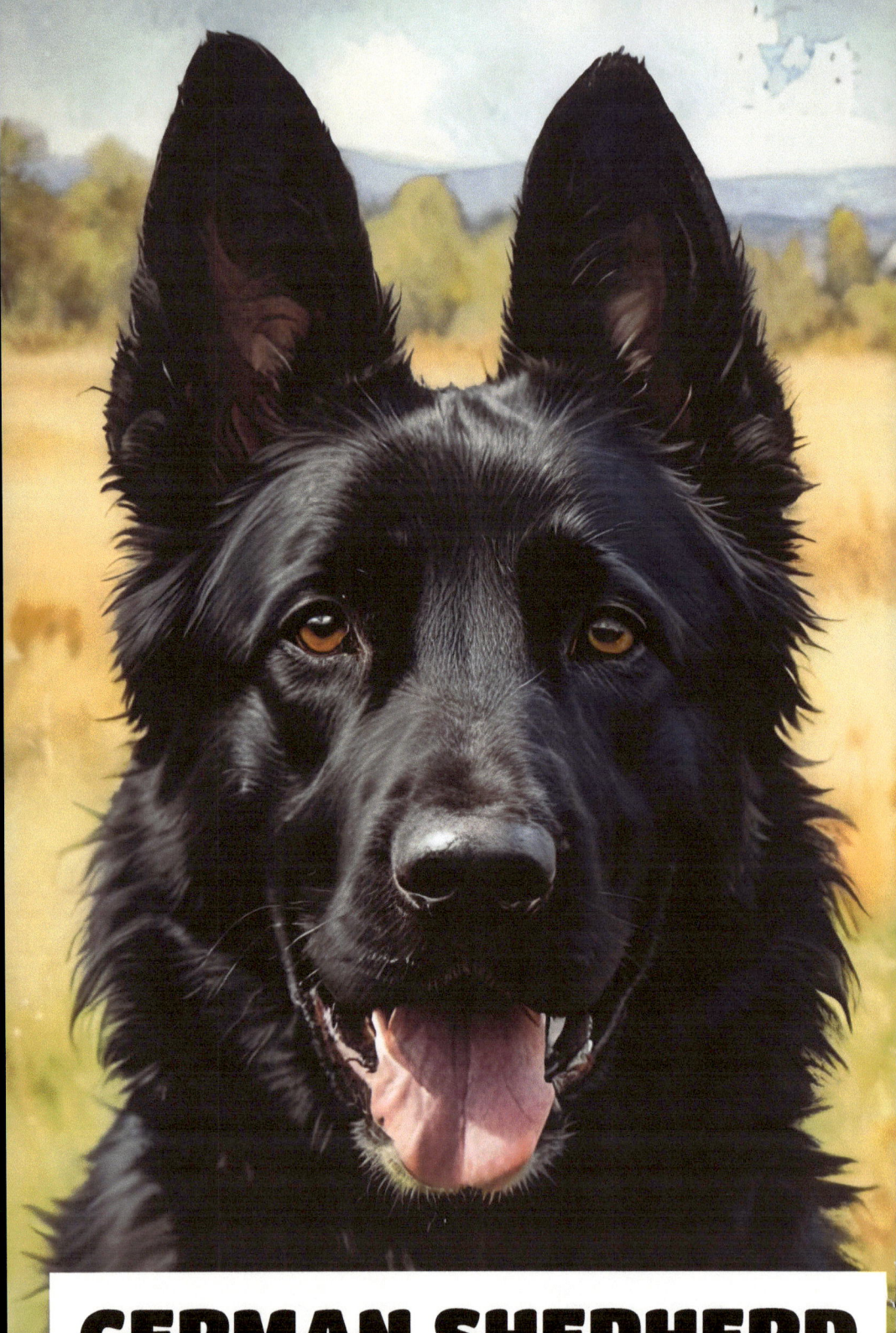

GERMAN SHEPHERD

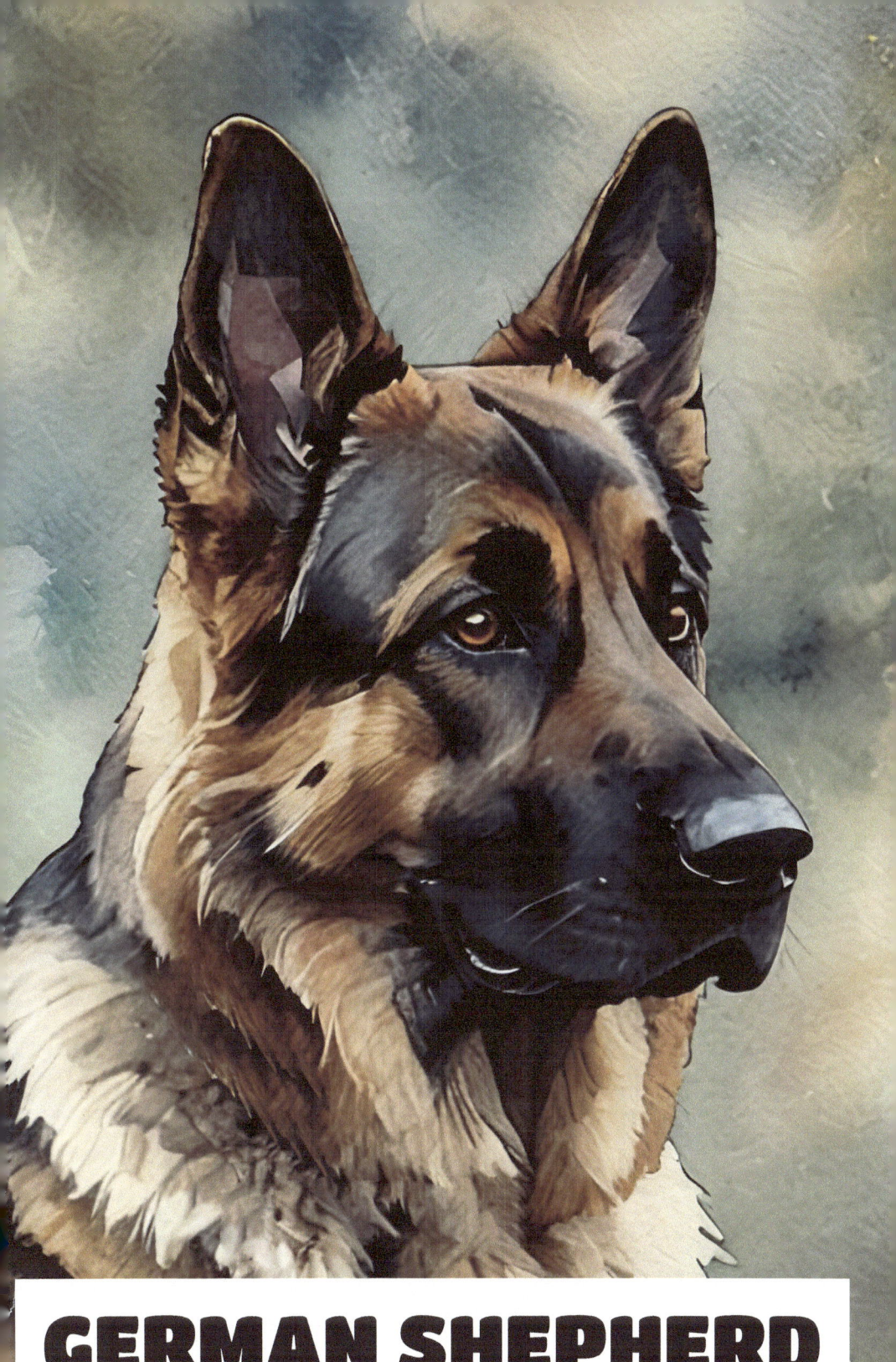

GERMAN SHEPHERD

www.ingramcontent.com/pod-product-compliance
Lightning Source LLC
Chambersburg PA
CBHW040253220526
45473CB00001B/465